1000 FACTS ABOUT FAMOUS FIGURES VOL. 1

© 2023, Daniel Scott

Contents

Introduction 8
Aaliyah (Singer, Actress) 9
Ada Lovelace (Mathematician) 10
Aesop (Fabulist) 11
Akira Kurosawa (Film Director) 12
Aldous Huxley (Writer) 13
Alexander Graham Bell (Inventor)............................. 14
Alfred Nobel (Chemist, Inventor) 15
Amitabh Bachchan (Actor) 16
Angela Davis (Activist) 17
Annie Leibovitz (Photographer) 19
Arthur Conan Doyle (Writer) 20
Audrey Hepburn (Actress) 21
Barack Obama (Politician) 22
Benedict Cumberbatch (Actor) 23
Billie Holiday (Singer) 24
Bob Marley (Singer-Songwriter) 25
Brad Pitt (Actor) 27
Bruce Lee (Actor, Martial Artist) 28
Béla Bartók (Composer) 29
Carl Sagan (Astronomer) 30
Catherine the Great (Ruler) 32
Charles Darwin (Naturalist) 33

Che Guevara (Revolutionary) 34
Chris Kyle (Military Sniper) 35
Claude Monet (Painter) 36
Coco Chanel (Fashion Designer) 37
Corazon Aquino (Politician) 38
David Bowie (Singer-Songwriter) 40
Desmond Tutu (Bishop) 41
Dmitri Shostakovich (Composer) 42
Douglas MacArthur (General) 43
Dwight D. Eisenhower (Politician) 44
Elizabeth I (Ruler) 45
Elvis Presley (Singer) 46
Emperor Nero (Ruler) 48
Ernest Hemingway (Writer) 49
Eva Perón (Politician) 50
Ferdinand Magellan (Explorer) 51
Francis Bacon (Philosopher) 53
Frank Lloyd Wright (Architect) 54
Franz Kafka (Writer) 55
Galileo Galilei (Astronomer) 56
George Harrison (Musician) 57
Georgia O'Keeffe (Painter) 58
Mahatma Gandhi (Activist) 59
Grace Hopper (Computer Scientist) 61
Greta Garbo (Actress) 62

Guy Fawkes (Revolutionary) 63
H.P. Lovecraft (Writer) 64
Harriet Tubman (Abolitionist) 65
Harry S. Truman (Politician) 67
Helen Keller (Author) 68
Henry VIII (Ruler) 69
Hippocrates (Physician) 70
Hubert de Givenchy (Fashion Designer) 71
Isaac Asimov (Writer) 72
Ivan the Terrible (Ruler) 74
Jackie Robinson (Baseball Player) 75
James Dean (Actor) 76
Janis Joplin (Singer) 77
Jim Henson (Puppeteer) 78
Joan of Arc (Military Leader) 80
Johannes Kepler (Astronomer) 81
John Locke (Philosopher) 82
Joseph Stalin (Politician) 83
Julia Child (Chef) 85
Katharine Hepburn (Actress) 86
Søren Kierkegaard (Philosopher) 87
King Tutankhamun (Pharaoh) 88
Lata Mangeshkar (Singer) 90
Leonardo da Vinci (Artist) 91
Lin-Manuel Miranda (Composer, Lyricist) 92

Lucille Ball (Actress) 93

Mahatma Gandhi (Activist) 94

Marco Polo (Explorer) 95

Maria Callas (Opera Singer) 97

Mark Twain (Writer) 98

Mary Shelley (Writer) 99

Maya Angelou (Writer) 100

Mickey Mantle (Baseball Player) 101

Mozart (Composer) 102

Nat King Cole (Singer) 104

Nikola Tesla (Inventor) 105

Oprah Winfrey (Media Mogul) 106

Otto von Bismarck (Politician) 107

Patsy Cline (Singer) 109

Peter Sellers (Actor) 110

Queen Elizabeth II (Monarch) 111

Rachel Carson (Marine Biologist) 112

Rembrandt (Painter) 113

Rita Hayworth (Actress) 114

Robert Oppenheimer (Physicist) 115

Rumi (Poet) 116

Samuel Beckett (Playwright) 117

Sigmund Freud (Psychologist) 119

Søren Kierkegaard (Philosopher) 120

Søren Kierkegaard (Philosopher) 121

Henri de Toulouse-Lautrec (Painter) 122
Walt Disney (Animator) 123
William Shakespeare (Playwright) 124
Conclusion 126

"A man is but the product of his thoughts. What he thinks, he becomes."
— Mahatma Gandhi

Introduction

Welcome to the first volume of an incredible journey, "1000 Facts About Famous Figures Vol. 1". This book invites you on a voyage of discovery, revealing lesser-known aspects of historical figures who have shaped our world. From the mysterious allure of artists to the logic-driven minds of scientists, from the persuasive power of politicians to the profound wisdom of philosophers, we present a diverse array of individuals and their extraordinary achievements.

Our intention is not merely to recapitulate well-known events or milestones, but rather to illuminate the human essence that lies beneath these accomplishments. What were their quirks? What little-known decisions led to their most impactful actions? This volume peels back the layers of each personality, granting us a peek into the inner workings of greatness.

As you delve into these pages, anticipate an enlightening encounter with the resilience, innovation, courage, and sheer brilliance of these influential figures. The aim of this book is to become a bridge, connecting you with the compelling narratives that collectively narrate the fascinating saga of human history and achievement. So, let's embark together on this adventure, ready to be surprised, inspired, and to gain a profound appreciation of what it truly means to impact the world.

Daniel Scott

Aaliyah (Singer, Actress)

- **Early Stardom:** Aaliyah signed her first record deal with Jive Records at only 12 years old.
- **Fashion Influencer:** Aaliyah's signature baggy pants and crop tops became a significant trend in the 90s, and she is often credited as a fashion influencer of the decade.
- **Multitalented:** Aaliyah was not just a successful singer but also a promising actress, starring in two films, "Romeo Must Die" and "Queen of the Damned."
- **High School with Superstars:** Aaliyah attended the Detroit High School for the Fine and Performing Arts with future stars like jazz singer Regina Carter.
- **Record Breaking:** Her second album, "One in a Million," became one of the first albums to reach "double platinum" status, selling over 3 million copies.
- **Named After Royalty:** Her name, Aaliyah, means 'highest, most exalted one' in Swahili, a fitting name for a music royalty.
- **Gone Too Soon:** Tragically, Aaliyah died in a plane crash in the Bahamas at the age of 22.
- **Unreleased Music:** Even after her death, her label has continued to release new music that Aaliyah had recorded but not released.
- **Star-studded Funeral:** Aaliyah's funeral was attended by many celebrities, and her casket was carried in a horse-drawn glass hearse.
- **Tributes:** Many artists, including Drake, Chris Brown, and Frank Ocean, have sampled Aaliyah's music in their songs as a tribute to her legacy.

Ada Lovelace (Mathematician)

- **First Programmer:** Lovelace is credited with writing instructions for the first computer program in the mid-1800s.
- **Famous Parentage:** She was the only legitimate child of poet Lord Byron, though she never knew him as he left England when she was just a few months old.
- **Prominent Tutor:** As a teenager, Lovelace was tutored by Augustus De Morgan, one of the greatest British mathematicians of her time.
- **Visionary Insight:** She was the first to recognize that Charles Babbage's proposed mechanical general-purpose computer, the Analytical Engine, had applications beyond pure calculation and published the first algorithm intended for implementation on it.
- **Babbage's Enchantress:** Charles Babbage, the inventor of the machine for which she wrote her programs, called Lovelace the "Enchantress of Numbers."
- **Math Over Poetry:** Despite her father being a famous poet, Lovelace's mother insisted she be tutored in math and science to avoid her developing her father's unpredictable temperament.
- **Gambler:** Lovelace loved to gamble and even tried to create a mathematical model for winning bets; unfortunately, her efforts failed and led to massive debt.
- **Early Death:** Lovelace died of uterine cancer at the age of 36, the same age at which her father had died.
- **Honoring Her Legacy:** The computer language "Ada," created by the U.S. Department of Defense, was named after Lovelace.

- **Ada Lovelace Day:** Celebrated in mid-October, Ada Lovelace Day promotes the achievements of women in science, technology, engineering, and maths (STEM).

Aesop (Fabulist)

- **Slave to Scholar:** Aesop was born a slave but earned his freedom through his cleverness and wit, according to ancient accounts.
- **Unsure Existence:** While his fables are well-known, there's debate among historians about whether Aesop actually existed or is a fictional character.
- **Worldwide Influence:** His fables, known as Aesop's Fables, have been translated into virtually every language in the world.
- **Art of Storytelling:** Aesop is believed to have invented the genre of fable, making animals the characters in his stories.
- **Death by Temple:** According to one ancient account, Aesop met an ironic end for a fabulist – he was thrown off a cliff after stealing a valuable cup from a temple.
- **Statue in Delphi:** The people of Delphi were so grateful for Aesop's defense of them that they erected a statue in his honor.
- **Aesop and Socrates:** The philosopher Socrates is said to have spent his time in prison turning Aesop's fables into verse.
- **Misattributed Fables:** Many fables from different cultures and periods have been incorrectly attributed to Aesop over the centuries.

- **Not Just for Children:**While often used for children's moral education, Aesop's Fables were originally told for adult audiences.
- **The Tortoise and the Hare:**Perhaps his most famous fable, "The Tortoise and the Hare," continues to be a universal symbol for the victory of perseverance and tenacity over arrogance and speed.

Akira Kurosawa (Film Director)

- **International Acclaim:**Kurosawa is one of the most important and influential filmmakers in the history of cinema, bringing Japanese cinema onto the global stage.
- **Inspiration for Star Wars:**His film "The Hidden Fortress" greatly influenced George Lucas and provided the narrative framework for "Star Wars."
- **Painting Passion:**Kurosawa initially aspired to be a painter before moving into film, and his love of painting influenced his visual style in cinema.
- **Survived Bombing:**He survived the Great Kanto Earthquake in 1923 and the bombing of Tokyo in World War II.
- **Shakespeare Adaptations:**Kurosawa directed cinematic adaptations of several Shakespeare plays, including "Macbeth" ("Throne of Blood") and "King Lear" ("Ran").
- **Prolific Career:**Over his career, he directed 30 films in 57 years.
- **Dreams into Film:**His film "Dreams" (1990) consists of 8 segments based on Kurosawa's actual dreams.

- **Honorary Award:** Kurosawa received an Honorary Award at the 1990 Academy Awards for his cinematic accomplishments.
- **Collaborations with Mifune:** Actor Toshiro Mifune, who starred in 16 of Kurosawa's films, was one of his most frequent collaborators.
- **Famed for Epic Narratives:** His most famous films, including "Seven Samurai," "Rashomon," and "Yojimbo," are celebrated for their epic narratives, memorable characters, and innovative techniques.

Aldous Huxley (Writer)

- **Brave New World:** Huxley is most well-known for his dystopian novel "Brave New World," which explores a future society built on technological comfort and control.
- **Visual Impairment:** An illness in his youth left Huxley nearly blind for a couple of years, and he had impaired vision for the rest of his life.
- **Psychedelics Proponent:** Huxley was an early advocate for the use of psychedelic substances, believing they could provide profound insights.
- **Hollywood Screenwriter:** Later in his career, Huxley moved to Hollywood and became a screenwriter, even writing an early draft for Disney's "Alice in Wonderland."
- **Final Hours:** On his deathbed, unable to speak, Huxley made a written request to his wife Laura for "LSD, 100 µg, intramuscular."

- **Coincidental Death:**Huxley died on the same day as President John F. Kennedy and fellow author C.S. Lewis - November 22, 1963.
- **Prolific Essayist:**Besides his novels, Huxley wrote numerous essays on philosophy, arts, society, and other topics.
- **The Doors of Perception:**Huxley's book "The Doors of Perception," detailing his experiences with mescaline, inspired the name of the band "The Doors."
- **Predictive Power:**Huxley's writings often accurately predicted technological and societal changes, such as the proliferation of mood-enhancing drugs and genetic engineering.
- **Pacifist:**Huxley was a committed pacifist, a stance that became particularly significant during the two World Wars.

Alexander Graham Bell (Inventor)

- **Telephone Inventor:**Bell is best known for his invention of the telephone, which transformed global communication.
- **Elocutionist:**Bell's mother and wife were both deaf, which influenced his research related to hearing and speech and led him to become an expert elocutionist.
- **National Geographic Society:**Bell served as the second president of the National Geographic Society and helped develop its first magazines.
- **Polyglot:**Bell spoke English, French, German, Italian, and Gaelic, and even developed his own family sign language.

- **Aerial Experiment Association:** Bell co-founded the Aerial Experiment Association, which made significant early advances in aviation.
- **Bell Labs:** After Bell's death, his company eventually became the modern telecommunication giant, Bell Laboratories.
- **Photo-phone Invention:** Bell also invented the photo-phone, which transmitted sound on a beam of light, a precursor to modern fiber optics.
- **Tesla Connection:** Bell's laboratory employed a young Nikola Tesla, another prominent inventor of the time.
- **First Transcontinental Call:** In 1915, Bell made the first transcontinental telephone call from New York to his assistant, Watson, in San Francisco.
- **Inventive Family:** Bell came from an inventive family; his grandfather invented a method for teaching speech to the deaf, and his father created a phonetic alphabet known as Visible Speech.

Alfred Nobel (Chemist, Inventor)

- **Dynamite Inventor:** Alfred Nobel is best known for inventing dynamite, which revolutionized construction, mining, and warfare.
- **Multi-lingual:** Nobel was fluent in several languages, including Swedish, Russian, French, English, and German.
- **Prolific Inventor:** Nobel held 355 different patents, making him one of the most prolific inventors in history.
- **Premature Obituary:** A French newspaper once published Nobel's obituary prematurely, calling him the "merchant of death" due to his invention of dynamite.

- **Nobel Prizes:** In response to his unwanted legacy as a "merchant of death," Nobel left the majority of his fortune to establish the Nobel Prizes, which honor advancements in physics, chemistry, medicine, literature, and peace.
- **Nitroglycerin Accidents:** Nobel's interest in explosives came from his family's involvement in the construction industry and was further heightened after his younger brother was killed in a nitroglycerin explosion.
- **Synthetic Rubber and Silk:** Apart from explosives, Nobel also made significant advancements in the development of synthetic rubber and silk.
- **Unmarried Life:** Despite having a few relationships, Nobel never married; his personal letters revealed a melancholic and lonely individual.
- **Workaholic:** Nobel was known to work up to 16 hours a day, even into his old age.
- **World Traveler:** Due to his work and multiple businesses, Nobel traveled widely and maintained homes in Paris, San Remo, and Stockholm.

Amitabh Bachchan (Actor)

- **Bollywood's Star:** Amitabh Bachchan is regarded as one of the greatest and most influential actors in the history of Indian cinema.
- **Towering Presence:** Known for his deep baritone voice and towering height (he stands at 6'2", quite tall by Indian standards), he earned the nickname "Angry Young Man" for his roles in Hindi cinema.

- **Near-Death Experience:** Bachchan almost lost his life during the filming of the movie "Coolie" in 1982 when he suffered a severe intestinal injury during a fight scene.
- **Reinvention:** Despite early struggles with failed ventures and bankruptcy in the 1990s, Bachchan successfully reinvented himself and remains active in cinema and television.
- **Famous Family:** He's married to actress Jaya Bhaduri, and their son Abhishek Bachchan and daughter-in-law Aishwarya Rai are also famous actors in Bollywood.
- **Television Success:** Bachchan has enjoyed success on television as the long-time host of India's version of the game show "Who Wants to Be a Millionaire?" ("Kaun Banega Crorepati").
- **Generous Philanthropist:** Bachchan is known for his philanthropic activities, including supporting causes like education and health for the underprivileged.
- **Multiple Awards:** He has won numerous awards in his career, including four National Film Awards for Best Actor and many awards at international film festivals.
- **Friend of the Gandhi Family:** Bachchan was a close friend of the Gandhi family and even briefly entered politics in support of long-time family friend, Rajiv Gandhi, before eventually deciding that politics was not for him.
- **Animated Avatar:** An animated version of Bachchan, known as "Astra Force," appeared in a superhero series on Indian television, showcasing his broad appeal across generations.

Angela Davis (Activist)

- **Political Activism:** Angela Davis became widely known as a radical African-American educator and activist for civil rights and other social issues in the 1960s.
- **Communist Party:** She was a member of the Communist Party USA, highlighting her commitment to socioeconomic equality.
- **Black Panther Party:** Davis had affiliations with the Black Panther Party, a revolutionary organization focused on the empowerment of the Black community.
- **High-Profile Trial:** She was arrested and charged with murder, kidnapping, and conspiracy due to her alleged involvement in a violent courthouse incident, but was acquitted in a high-profile trial.
- **Run for Vice President:** Davis ran as the vice presidential candidate on the Communist Party USA ticket in 1980 and 1984.
- **Academic Pursuits:** She was a professor at the University of California, Santa Cruz, where she taught courses on the history of consciousness.
- **Feminism Advocate:** Davis was one of the founders of the intersectional feminist organization, the National Alliance Against Racist and Political Repression.
- **Prison Industrial Complex:** She is known for her critiques of the "prison-industrial complex," and is a founding member of Critical Resistance, a national organization dedicated to dismantling the prison system.
- **Authorship:** Davis is an accomplished author, having written several books on class, feminism, and the U.S. prison system.
- **Continued Activism:** Even in her seventies, Davis remains a vocal activist, speaking on issues such as prison reform, racial disparities, and gender equality.

Annie Leibovitz (Photographer)

- **Rolling Stone:** Annie Leibovitz began her career as a staff photographer for Rolling Stone magazine, eventually becoming its chief photographer.
- **Iconic Shots:** She is responsible for some of the most iconic celebrity photographs of the 20th and 21st century, including a naked John Lennon curled around Yoko Ono, shot hours before his assassination.
- **First Woman:** Leibovitz was the first woman to have an exhibition at Washington's National Portrait Gallery in 1991.
- **Collaboration:** Leibovitz has often collaborated with famous subjects to create more insightful and personal portraits.
- **Commercials:** Beyond her work in print, she's also known for directing a number of high-profile advertising campaigns.
- **Books:** She has published several books that compile her photographs, including "Annie Leibovitz: Photographs" and "Women."
- **Disney Dream:** She took the famous Disney Dream Portrait series, transforming celebrities into Disney characters.
- **Vanity Fair:** Since 1983, Leibovitz has been a contributing photographer for Vanity Fair, where many of her most famous images have been published.
- **Personal Life:** Her life and work have been the subject of film and television productions, including the documentary "Annie Leibovitz: Life Through a Lens."

- **Influence:**She has been cited as an inspiration by many other successful photographers for her innovative and personal style.

Arthur Conan Doyle (Writer)

- **Sherlock Holmes Creator:**Doyle is best known for creating the legendary detective Sherlock Holmes, whose stories are considered milestones in the field of crime fiction.
- **Doctor Turned Writer:**Before becoming a successful author, Doyle studied medicine at the University of Edinburgh and even based the character of Sherlock Holmes on his university professor, Dr. Joseph Bell.
- **Voluminous Output:**Doyle authored more than 60 Sherlock Holmes stories, along with several novels, poems, and historical works.
- **Spiritualism Advocate:**Later in life, Doyle developed a strong interest in spiritualism and psychic phenomena, and he wrote and lectured extensively on the subject.
- **War Veteran:**He served as a surgeon in the Second Boer War, and his experiences led him to write "The War in South Africa: Its Cause and Conduct," which defended British actions in the war.
- **Knighthood:**Doyle was knighted in 1902, not for his literary work, but for his pamphlet on the Boer War.
- **Holmes' Popularity:**Despite his numerous other works, Doyle was continually drawn back to Sherlock Holmes due to the character's immense popularity, even after he famously "killed off" Holmes in "The Final Problem."

- **Sports Enthusiast:** An avid sportsman, Doyle played football, cricket, and golf, and he even helped popularize skiing in Switzerland.
- **Amateur Detective:** Taking a cue from his famous character, Doyle sometimes used his deductive skills in real life. In one case, he helped overturn the convictions of two individuals who were wrongly accused.
- **The Hound:** Doyle's novel "The Hound of the Baskervilles" was inspired by the legend of a fearsome, ghostly hound in Dartmoor, the area where he often went for holidays.

Audrey Hepburn (Actress)

- **War Survivor:** Audrey Hepburn endured hardships during the Nazi occupation of the Netherlands in World War II, an experience that profoundly affected her later life and humanitarian work.
- **Ballet Dreams:** Prior to her acting career, Hepburn was an aspiring ballerina, but her dreams were thwarted by her malnutrition during the war.
- **Hollywood Icon:** Audrey Hepburn became an icon of Hollywood's Golden Age, remembered for her roles in classic films like 'Breakfast at Tiffany's,' 'Roman Holiday,' and 'My Fair Lady.'
- **Fashion Icon:** Hepburn was a muse of designer Hubert de Givenchy and popularized the 'little black dress' in 'Breakfast at Tiffany's,' making her a lasting fashion icon.

- **EGOT Achiever:** Hepburn is one of the few people to have won an Emmy, Grammy, Oscar, and Tony award – the coveted EGOT.
- **Innocence Appeal:** Hepburn was known for her distinctive innocent charm, a characteristic that set her apart in an era of sultry screen sirens.
- **Humanitarian Work:** After retiring from acting, Hepburn devoted herself to humanitarian work as a Goodwill Ambassador for UNICEF, focusing on children's issues around the world.
- **Unique Honor:** She was posthumously awarded the Presidential Medal of Freedom for her work with UNICEF, an honor rarely given to entertainers.
- **Garden Rose:** A breed of rose was named after Hepburn in recognition of her life and career, known as the Audrey Hepburn rose.
- **Timeless Legacy:** Audrey Hepburn's legacy continues to inspire new generations, making her one of the most enduring icons of both classic cinema and humanitarian work.

Barack Obama (Politician)

- **Mixed Heritage:** Obama is of Kenyan (father) and American (mother) descent, making his upbringing a blend of cultures.
- **Historical Presidency:** He made history in 2008 by becoming the first African-American President of the United States.
- **Nobel Laureate:** In 2009, Obama was awarded the Nobel Peace Prize for his extraordinary efforts to

strengthen international diplomacy and cooperation between peoples.
- **Healthcare Reform:** His administration introduced the Affordable Care Act (commonly known as Obamacare), a major reform in U.S. healthcare.
- **Childhood Abroad:** He spent part of his childhood in Jakarta, Indonesia, providing him with a global perspective from an early age.
- **Harvard Law:** He made history at Harvard Law School by becoming the first African-American president of the prestigious Harvard Law Review.
- **Grammy Winner:** Surprisingly, Obama is a two-time Grammy Award winner, both for spoken word albums of his memoirs.
- **Basketball Enthusiast:** He is a fervent basketball fan, often seen playing with staff during his presidency and prominently supporting the Chicago Bulls.
- **Name Meaning:** His first name, Barack, means "one who is blessed" in Swahili.
- **Post-Presidency:** Post-presidency, he has been active in various community service activities and has also ventured into film and TV production with his wife, Michelle, through their company, Higher Ground Productions.

Benedict Cumberbatch (Actor)

- **Sherlock Holmes:** Cumberbatch skyrocketed to fame for his portrayal of Sherlock Holmes in BBC's "Sherlock," bringing a modern twist to the classic detective.

- **Name Change:** As a young actor, he considered using a stage name because he worried that "Cumberbatch" sounded too foppish.
- **Eccentric Roles:** He has a penchant for portraying complex, brilliant, and often eccentric characters, including real-life figures like Alan Turing in "The Imitation Game."
- **Classically Trained:** He's a classically trained actor and has performed in various Shakespearean plays, including "Hamlet."
- **Diverse Talents:** His talents extend beyond acting; he has also narrated numerous audiobooks and documentaries.
- **Marvel Hero:** He portrays Doctor Strange in the Marvel Cinematic Universe, a role that required him to learn sleight of hand tricks from professional magicians.
- **Kidnapping Survival:** While filming in South Africa in 2005, Cumberbatch and two colleagues were abducted; they were later released unharmed.
- **Philanthropy:** He's an ambassador for multiple charities and used his fame to raise awareness for various causes, including mental health and refugees' rights.
- **Awards:** He's been nominated for numerous awards, including an Academy Award for Best Actor, and won an Emmy for his role in "Sherlock."
- **Royal Connection:** Cumberbatch is a distant relative of King Richard III; he read a poem at the king's reburial ceremony in 2015.

Billie Holiday (Singer)

- **Jazz Icon:** Billie Holiday, often referred to as "Lady Day," is one of the most influential jazz vocalists of all time.
- **Songstress of Sorrow:** She was known for her deeply emotive and personal singing style, often interpreting songs with a sense of tragedy and melancholy.
- **Difficult Childhood:** Holiday had a difficult childhood that included working as a prostitute in her early teenage years before she discovered her musical talent.
- **Signature Song:** Her haunting rendition of "Strange Fruit," a song about lynching in the American South, is considered one of the most powerful protest songs ever recorded.
- **Grammy Hall of Fame:** Multiple recordings of hers, including "God Bless the Child" and "Strange Fruit," have been inducted into the Grammy Hall of Fame.
- **Carnegie Hall:** Despite personal and legal struggles, she performed to a sold-out crowd at Carnegie Hall in 1948, a significant achievement for any artist.
- **Autobiography:** Her autobiography, "Lady Sings the Blues," tells the raw and painful story of her life, though some have questioned its accuracy.
- **Untimely Death:** Holiday died at the age of 44 due to complications from drug and alcohol abuse.
- **Posthumous Honors:** In 1987, she was posthumously awarded the Grammy Lifetime Achievement Award.
- **Statue Tribute:** A statue of Holiday was erected in Baltimore, Maryland, her place of birth, in 2009.

Bob Marley (Singer-Songwriter)

- **Global Icon:**Bob Marley, a Jamaican singer-songwriter, became a global cultural icon for his pioneering of reggae music and his Rastafarian faith.
- **Reggae Legend:**Marley's music was deeply intertwined with his socio-political insights and his steadfast belief in the power of love and unity.
- **Universal Message:**Songs like "One Love," "Three Little Birds," and "Redemption Song" carried messages of peace, love, and resistance to oppression that continue to resonate globally.
- **Wailers Band:**He was a part of the band, 'The Wailers', which produced reggae classics like "I Shot the Sheriff" and "No Woman, No Cry".
- **Exile Period:**After a failed assassination attempt in Jamaica, Marley spent two years in self-imposed exile in England where he produced the hit album 'Exodus'.
- **Love for Soccer:**Marley was a passionate football player and followed the sport closely throughout his life.
- **Religious Beliefs:**As a devout Rastafarian, Marley strongly believed in the use of marijuana as a sacrament and for its medicinal properties.
- **Honors:**Marley was posthumously inducted into the Rock and Roll Hall of Fame in 1994.
- **"Legend" Album:**His greatest hits album, "Legend", released three years after his death, is reggae's best-selling album, going ten times Platinum in the U.S.
- **Cultural Ambassador:**More than three decades after his death from cancer at age 36, Marley remains the most widely recognized and influential figure in reggae music history.

Brad Pitt (Actor)

- **Origins:** Born in Oklahoma and raised in Missouri, Brad Pitt is known for his Midwestern charm.
- **Breakthrough Role:** He achieved recognition for his cowboy hitchhiker role in the film "Thelma & Louise" (1991).
- **Versatile Actor:** Pitt's roles have spanned various genres, from romantic leads in "Legends of the Fall" (1994) and "Meet Joe Black" (1998) to gritty roles in "Fight Club" (1999) and "Inglourious Basterds" (2009).
- **Oscar Winner:** He won his first acting Oscar for Best Supporting Actor for his role in "12 Monkeys" (1995) and his first Best Actor Oscar for "Once Upon a Time in Hollywood" (2019).
- **Producer:** Beyond acting, Pitt is also a successful film producer with his company, Plan B Entertainment, having produced Oscar-winning films like "The Departed" (2006) and "12 Years a Slave" (2013).
- **Architecture:** Pitt has a strong interest in architecture and founded the Make It Right Foundation, which builds sustainable homes in areas devastated by Hurricane Katrina.
- **Humanitarian Efforts:** He is well known for his humanitarian and political activism, particularly his work with the ONE Campaign, Make It Right Foundation, and Jolie-Pitt Foundation.
- **Personal Life:** His high-profile relationships with Jennifer Aniston and Angelina Jolie, as well as his fatherhood to six children, have made him a constant fixture in celebrity news.
- **Awards:** Throughout his career, he has received multiple awards, including two Golden Globe Awards

and an Academy Award for his acting, in addition to another Academy Award as a producer under his own company, Plan B Entertainment.
- **Net Worth:** As of my knowledge cutoff in 2021, Brad Pitt's net worth is estimated to be approximately $300 million.

Bruce Lee (Actor, Martial Artist)

- **Birth:** Bruce Lee was born on November 27, 1940, in San Francisco, California, while his parents were on tour with a Chinese opera.
- **Name:** His birth name was Lee Jun-fan, but he was given the English name "Bruce" by a nurse at his birth hospital.
- **Child Actor:** Lee began his acting career as a child in Hong Kong, appearing in over 20 films before the age of 18.
- **Martial Arts:** He started learning martial arts at the age of 13 and later developed his own martial arts philosophy that became known as Jeet Kune Do.
- **Breakthrough:** He gained international fame for his role in the TV series "The Green Hornet" (1966–1967) and later for his roles in major films such as "Fists of Fury" and "Enter the Dragon".
- **Physical Feats:** Lee was known for his amazing physical feats, including his famous one-inch punch and two-finger push-ups.
- **Philosophy:** Lee wrote extensively, expressing his views not only on martial arts but also on life, acting, and self-realization.

- **Untimely Death:** He died at the age of 32 on July 20, 1973, due to a reaction to a painkiller, leaving behind a massive cultural legacy.
- **Legacy:** His influence on martial arts, both on screen and in practice, has been enormous, making him a cultural icon.
- **Influence:** Lee is considered by many to be the most influential martial artist of all time and a pop culture figure of the 20th century.

Béla Bartók (Composer)

- **Birth:** Béla Bartók was born on March 25, 1881, in the small Banatian town of Nagyszentmiklós in the Kingdom of Hungary, Austria-Hungary (present-day Sânnicolau Mare, Romania).
- **Musical Prodigy:** Bartók exhibited extraordinary musical talent from a very young age, giving his first public concert, featuring a piece he composed himself, at the age of 11.
- **Education:** He studied piano and composition at the Royal Academy of Music in Budapest, where he later returned as a faculty member.
- **Folk Music:** Bartók had a lifelong passion for Hungarian folk music, which he incorporated into his compositions. He also pioneered the field of ethnomusicology by collecting and transcribing folk songs from across Central Europe.
- **Compositions:** His notable works include six string quartets, the opera "Duke Bluebeard's Castle," the ballet "The Miraculous Mandarin," and the orchestral

works "Concerto for Orchestra" and "Music for Strings, Percussion, and Celesta."
- **Style:** Bartók's music is characterized by complex rhythms, rich harmonies, and an innovative synthesis of folk and classical traditions.
- **Move to America:** He immigrated to the United States in 1940 due to the outbreak of World War II and the rise of the Nazis. In America, he struggled to find a stable source of income but continued to compose.
- **Posthumous Recognition:** While Bartók's music was initially received with hesitation due to its unique and complex nature, he gained wider recognition after his death, with many considering him one of the most significant composers of the 20th century.
- **Legacy:** Bartók left a significant legacy in both classical music and the field of ethnomusicology. His research into folk music greatly influenced both his own compositions and the wider field of musicology.
- **Death:** Béla Bartók passed away on September 26, 1945, in New York City, due to complications from leukemia. His body was later reinterred in Budapest, Hungary, in 1988.

Carl Sagan (Astronomer)

- **Cosmic Communicator:** Carl Sagan was not just a leading astronomer but also an incredibly successful science communicator, making the complexities of the universe understandable to millions through his books and TV show.
- **Star-studded Teacher:** Sagan was a professor of astronomy at Cornell University where he influenced a

generation of scientists, including notable astrophysicist Neil deGrasse Tyson.
- **Cosmos Creator:** He wrote and hosted "Cosmos: A Personal Voyage," a hugely popular 13-part television series exploring the universe and our place in it.
- **Extraterrestrial Messenger:** Sagan played an integral role in the creation of the Voyager Golden Records, which contain sounds and images of Earth intended for any extraterrestrial beings who might encounter the Voyager spacecrafts.
- **Pulitzer Prize Recipient:** Sagan won the Pulitzer Prize for General Non-Fiction in 1978 for his book "The Dragons of Eden," which discussed the evolution of human intelligence.
- **Baloney Detection Kit:** Sagan devised a "Baloney Detection Kit" - a set of tools to critically evaluate any argument or line of reasoning.
- **Nuclear Winter Predictor:** Alongside his colleagues, Sagan developed the concept of "nuclear winter", a severe and prolonged global climatic cooling effect hypothesized to occur after widespread firestorms following a nuclear war.
- **Martian Expert:** Sagan contributed to the first successful missions to Mars, performed by both NASA's Mariner and Viking spacecraft.
- **Famous Phrase Coiner:** He popularized the phrase "We are made of star stuff" to explain that most of the elements that make up the human body and the Earth originated in stars.
- **Science Advocate:** Sagan was a tireless advocate for scientific skepticism and the scientific method, promoting critical and logical thinking in his works.

Catherine the Great (Ruler)

- **Empress Enigma:** Catherine the Great was actually not born Russian - she was born Sophie of Anhalt-Zerbst in Prussia, now Germany.
- **Language Legacy:** She learned Russian, converted to Russian Orthodoxy, and changed her name to Catherine (Yekaterina) to marry into the Russian royal family.
- **Throne Triumph:** She became the Empress of Russia after a successful coup d'état against her husband, Peter III, in 1762, ruling for 34 years until her death.
- **Enlightenment Era:** Catherine was an Enlightened despot, corresponding with philosophers like Voltaire and Diderot, and attempted to modernize Russia along Western European lines.
- **Culture Champion:** She was a patron of the arts, literature, and education, transforming her court in St. Petersburg into a hub of the European Enlightenment.
- **Territorial Triumph:** Under her rule, Russia expanded its territories significantly, even to Alaska, becoming one of the dominant powers in Europe.
- **Peasant Paradox:** Despite her Enlightenment ideals, Catherine implemented serfdom more extensively than any ruler before her, which significantly impacted the lower social classes.
- **Ornate Offspring:** Catherine the Great established the Hermitage Museum in Saint Petersburg, Russia. Today it houses one of the world's most extensive collections of art and culture.
- **Vaccine Vanguard:** Catherine was a proponent of smallpox vaccination, even getting inoculated herself to promote its use in Russia.

- **Rumor Ridicule:** Despite the many scandalous rumors that circulated about her personal life and death, Catherine the Great actually died of a stroke.

Charles Darwin (Naturalist)

- **Evolutionary Theory:** Charles Darwin is renowned for developing the theory of evolution, challenging centuries-old beliefs about the creation of life.
- **HMS Beagle Voyage:** His five-year voyage aboard the HMS Beagle in the 1830s, particularly his observations in the Galapagos Islands, were crucial to the development of his theory.
- **Origin of Species:** Darwin's most famous work, "On the Origin of Species," published in 1859, introduced the concept of natural selection, where species evolve over generations through a process of random mutation and survival of the fittest.
- **Delayed Publication:** Despite formulating his theory by the late 1830s, Darwin did not publish his findings for more than 20 years due to fear of criticism from the religious community.
- **Botanical Studies:** Darwin also conducted extensive studies in botany and was the first to explain the process of fertilization in plants.
- **The Darwin-Wallace Line:** The boundary separating the ecozones of Asia and Australia is named the Darwin–Wallace Line, commemorating Darwin and Alfred Russel Wallace, who independently conceived the theory of evolution through natural selection.

- **Family Life:** Darwin married his first cousin, Emma Wedgwood, and they had ten children together, three of whom died at an early age.
- **Ill Health:** Darwin suffered from chronic ill health throughout his adult life, possibly due to Chagas disease contracted during his travels.
- **Victorian Skepticism:** Despite initial skepticism in Victorian society, Darwin's theories became widely accepted among scientific circles by the time of his death in 1882.
- **Enduring Legacy:** Today, Darwin's theory of evolution forms the basis of modern biology, and he is considered one of the most influential figures in human history.

Che Guevara (Revolutionary)

- **Physician:** Before becoming a revolutionary, Ernesto "Che" Guevara was a trained and licensed physician, having studied at the University of Buenos Aires.
- **Motorcycle Diaries:** Guevara's continental motorcycle trip across South America when he was in his early 20s profoundly affected his worldview and political beliefs.
- **Cuban Revolution:** Guevara was a key figure in the Cuban Revolution, serving as Fidel Castro's right-hand man and playing a pivotal role in overthrowing the Batista regime in 1959.
- **Guerrilla Warfare:** Che Guevara wrote a manual on guerrilla warfare, detailing his theories and strategies for successful revolutions based on his experiences in Cuba.
- **United Nations:** Guevara represented Cuba at the United Nations General Assembly in 1964, delivering a

speech criticizing U.S. foreign policy and apartheid in South Africa.
- **Economic Role:** In Cuba's post-revolution government, Guevara served as the director of the nation's central bank and the minister of industry, attempting to steer the country toward a communist economic model.
- **Che:** The nickname "Che" comes from an Argentine interjection similar to "hey" or "mate", used frequently by Guevara.
- **Bolivia:** Guevara was captured and executed in Bolivia in 1967 while trying to incite a revolution similar to the one in Cuba.
- **Iconic Image:** The photo of Guevara, titled "Guerrillero Heroico" and taken by Alberto Korda, is considered one of the most iconic and widely reproduced images in the world.
- **Legacy:** Che Guevara remains a symbolic figure worldwide, seen as an emblem of rebellion and global counterculture, while his political and economic ideas continue to be the subject of debate and analysis.

Chris Kyle (Military Sniper)

- **Prolific Sniper:** Chris Kyle was a United States Navy SEAL and the most lethal sniper in U.S. military history with 160 confirmed kills out of 255 probable kills.
- **Tours of Duty:** Kyle served four tours in the Iraq War and was awarded several commendations for acts of heroism and meritorious service in combat.
- **Nicknames:** He was known as "The Devil of Ramadi" by insurgents and was so feared that there was an $80,000 bounty placed on his head.

- **Decorations:** His military awards include the Silver Star Medal, the Bronze Star Medal (four times), a Navy and Marine Corps Commendation Medal, and a Navy and Marine Corps Achievement Medal.
- **Best-Selling Author:** After retiring from the military, Kyle wrote a best-selling autobiography, 'American Sniper,' which was later turned into a movie directed by Clint Eastwood.
- **Transition Assistance:** Kyle was heavily involved in charities helping military veterans transition back into civilian life, and he helped establish the FITCO Cares Foundation.
- **Controversies:** Kyle's account of his military exploits has been both praised and questioned, with some of his claims disputed by fellow soldiers and journalists.
- **Personal Life:** Kyle was married to Taya Kyle, and they had two children together.
- **Tragic End:** Kyle was tragically killed at a shooting range in 2013 by a Marine veteran whom he was trying to help cope with post-traumatic stress disorder (PTSD).
- **Legacy:** Despite controversies surrounding his life, Kyle's impact on American military history and veteran support has been significant, and he continues to be a subject of books and films.

Claude Monet (Painter)

- **Impressionism Pioneer:** Claude Monet was one of the founding figures of the French Impressionist movement in the 19th century.

- **Lily Pads:** His series of Water Lilies paintings, made in his own garden, are some of his most famous works and symbolize the Impressionist style.
- **En Plein Air:** Monet was known for painting en plein air, a French term meaning "outdoors," which allowed him to capture natural light and color in his work.
- **Impression, Sunrise:** His painting 'Impression, Sunrise' gave the name to the Impressionist movement itself.
- **Series Painting:** Monet developed the practice of painting the same scene multiple times to capture the changing of light and the passing of the seasons.
- **Financial Struggles:** Despite being celebrated today, Monet struggled with poverty and depression for much of his life.
- **Giverny:** His home and garden at Giverny are now a major tourist attraction and museum, preserving his creative environment.
- **Eye Problems:** In his later years, Monet suffered from cataracts which greatly affected his painting, leading to a darker and redder palette.
- **Large Scale Works:** Monet's 'Water Lilies' series includes large scale works, some as wide as 6 meters, designed to immerse the viewer in the scene.
- **Legacy:** Monet's work has had a significant impact on the course of modern art and he is remembered as one of the greatest painters in history.

Coco Chanel (Fashion Designer)

- **Little Black Dress:** Coco Chanel revolutionized women's fashion in the 1920s with the introduction of

the "Little Black Dress," which is now a staple in most women's wardrobes.
- **Chanel No. 5:** She created the iconic Chanel No. 5 perfume, which was one of the first perfumes to use synthetic components rather than natural scents.
- **Orphanage Upbringing:** Chanel learned to sew while she was raised in an orphanage, which would later be instrumental in her success as a fashion designer.
- **Unconventional Designs:** Chanel rebelled against the corseted silhouette of the time and popularized a sporty, casual chic as the feminine standard of style.
- **Chanel Suit:** She is known for the creation of the "Chanel Suit," a women's suit made of wool with a collarless jacket and a well-fitted skirt.
- **Women's Pants:** Chanel played a significant role in popularizing pants for women, which was a radical change in the fashion world.
- **Self-Made:** Coco Chanel was a self-made woman who built one of the most powerful fashion empires in the world from scratch.
- **World War II Controversy:** Her legacy was clouded with controversy due to her association with a German officer during World War II.
- **Iconic Logo:** The Chanel brand's double-C logo is one of the most recognized logos in the global fashion industry.
- **Enduring Influence:** Chanel's influence on haute couture was such that she was the only person in the couturier field to be named on TIME Magazine's 100 most influential people of the 20th century.

Corazon Aquino (Politician)

- **Philippines' First Female President:** Corazon Aquino was the first female president of the Philippines, serving from 1986 to 1992.
- **People Power Revolution:** Aquino came into power after the 1986 People Power Revolution, which peacefully overthrew dictator Ferdinand Marcos.
- **Non-political Background:** She had no political experience before becoming president; she was thrust into the political arena following the assassination of her husband, Senator Benigno Aquino Jr.
- **Time's Woman of the Year:** In 1986, Time Magazine named her "Woman of the Year".
- **Democracy Restored:** Her administration was credited for restoring democratic institutions in the Philippines after the long dictatorship of Marcos.
- **Survived Coup Attempts:** During her presidency, Aquino survived several coup attempts against her government.
- **Reluctant Leader:** Aquino was often referred to as the "reluctant president" because she never desired the role, but took it up to fight the corruption and abuses of the Marcos regime.
- **Support for Non-violence:** Aquino's adherence to non-violence and negotiation made her a global symbol of peaceful resistance against oppressive regimes.
- **Historic Election:** Her presidential election was one of the most dramatic and attended in Philippine history, with widespread allegations of election tampering sparking the People Power Revolution.
- **Honoring Her Legacy:** To commemorate her role in bringing democracy back to the Philippines, her face and a quote from her 1986 speech are featured on the 500 Philippine peso bill.

David Bowie (Singer-Songwriter)

- **Chameleon of Rock:** Known as the "chameleon of rock" for his ability to change his style and appearance, Bowie had a career spanning over five decades, with continuous reinvention and visual presentation.
- **Iconic Personas:** Bowie created various alter-egos, such as Ziggy Stardust and the Thin White Duke, each characterized by unique musical styles and fashion statements.
- **One-of-a-kind Eye:** A schoolyard fight over a girl left Bowie with a permanently dilated pupil, giving him the appearance of having two different colored eyes.
- **Space Oddity:** Bowie's breakthrough hit "Space Oddity" was released just days before the Apollo 11 moon landing, cementing his association with cosmic themes.
- **Bowie Bonds:** In 1997, David Bowie made financial history by offering "Bowie Bonds" for sale, which allowed investors to buy shares in his future earnings.
- **Art Collector:** Bowie was an avid art collector, with a collection that ranged from contemporary African art to British 20th-century works and pieces from the Outsider Art movement.
- **Acting Career:** Besides music, Bowie also had an accomplished acting career, including notable roles in movies like "Labyrinth" and "The Man Who Fell to Earth."
- **Pioneering Web User:** An early adopter of the internet, Bowie launched his own internet service

- provider, BowieNet, in 1998, which offered users exclusive content.
- **Grammy Stardom:** In the wake of his death, Bowie's final album "Blackstar" won all five of its nominated categories at the 59th Annual Grammy Awards.
- **Berlin Legacy:** Bowie's time in West Berlin in the late '70s is immortalized with a commemorative plaque, and fans still flock to his old apartment to pay homage.

Desmond Tutu (Bishop)

- **Nobel Peace Prize:** Desmond Tutu received the Nobel Peace Prize in 1984 for his work combating apartheid in South Africa.
- **Groundbreaking:** He was the first Black Anglican Archbishop of both Cape Town and Johannesburg.
- **Truth and Reconciliation Commission:** Tutu chaired the Truth and Reconciliation Commission (TRC), a landmark body established to investigate human rights abuses during the apartheid era.
- **Distinctive Voice:** Tutu was known for his distinctively high-pitched, playful voice, which contrasted sharply with the gravitas of his messages.
- **Homosexuality Advocacy:** Despite facing opposition, Tutu was an outspoken advocate for the rights of the LGBTQ+ community within the Church and society at large.
- **Comic Book Character:** Tutu's fight against apartheid was featured in a comic book titled "Tutu's Children," released in the 1980s.

- **Social Media Activist:** Even in his late years, Tutu used social media platforms like Twitter to continue advocating for human rights and social justice.
- **Royal Connections:** In 2013, Tutu baptized the third in line to the British throne, Prince George.
- **Apartheid's Downfall:** Desmond Tutu is credited with coining the term "Rainbow Nation" as a metaphor to describe post-apartheid South Africa after the first democratic elections in 1994.
- **Honorary Degrees:** Tutu has been awarded numerous honorary degrees from prestigious universities around the world, including Harvard, Oxford, and Columbia.

Dmitri Shostakovich (Composer)

- **Prodigy:** Shostakovich was considered a child prodigy, entering the Petrograd Conservatory at just 13 years old.
- **Stalin's Shadow:** Much of Shostakovich's work was composed under the repressive Soviet regime of Joseph Stalin, greatly influencing his style and thematic choices.
- **Unorthodox Opera:** His opera, "Lady Macbeth of Mtsensk," was denounced by Stalin, forcing Shostakovich to withdraw his Fourth Symphony.
- **Symphonic Success:** Despite early criticism, Shostakovich went on to compose 15 symphonies, many of which are considered among the greatest of the 20th century.
- **War-time Composer:** His Seventh Symphony, known as the "Leningrad," was performed during the Siege of

Leningrad in World War II, becoming a symbol of Russian resistance.
- **Multifaceted Musician:**Shostakovich wasn't only a composer; he was also a renowned pianist and a skilled conductor.
- **Musical Messages:**Some believe Shostakovich's music contains hidden dissident messages criticizing the Soviet regime, a topic still debated among scholars.
- **Film Scorer:**Shostakovich composed music for around 36 films, showcasing his ability to adapt his style to different mediums.
- **Risky Reprieve:**After Stalin's death, Shostakovich felt free to compose his Thirteenth Symphony, "Babi Yar," which condemned anti-Semitism and the Soviet regime.
- **Sports Enthusiast:**Oddly enough, Shostakovich was a big fan of football and even penned an article titled "Soccer, Symphony, Lenin, and Me."

Douglas MacArthur (General)

- **Baseball Dreamer:**Before his military career, MacArthur had aspirations to play professional baseball and even tried out for the baseball team at West Point.
- **Medal of Honor:**MacArthur was one of only five men ever to rise to the rank of General of the Army in the U.S. Army, and the only man ever to become a field marshal in the Philippine Army, in addition to being a Medal of Honor recipient.
- **Youngest Superintendent:**At age 39, MacArthur became the youngest superintendent in history at the United States Military Academy at West Point.

- **Iconic Speech:** "I shall return," the promise MacArthur made to the Filipino people as he was forced to evacuate in the face of Japanese advances during World War II, is among the most famous quotes of the war.
- **Innovative Warfare:** He is known for his strategic "island-hopping" campaign, which played a major role in ending World War II.
- **Father-Son Duo:** MacArthur and his father, Arthur MacArthur, Jr., are one of only two pairs of father and son to have each been awarded a Medal of Honor.
- **Korean War Clash:** MacArthur clashed with President Truman over the handling of the Korean War, leading to his dismissal – a controversial decision at the time.
- **Post-War Japan:** He oversaw the occupation and reconstruction of Japan after World War II, including the drafting of a new constitution.
- **World War I Hero:** During World War I, MacArthur famously led the Rainbow Division and was nicknamed "the fightingest man" in the war.
- **Corncob Pipe:** MacArthur is often remembered for his signature corncob pipe, a personal quirk that became an iconic symbol of the general.

Dwight D. Eisenhower (Politician)

- **Military Career:** Before becoming the 34th President of the United States, Eisenhower was a five-star general in the U.S. Army during World War II.
- **D-Day:** As Supreme Commander of the Allied Forces in Europe, he masterminded the successful D-Day invasion of Normandy.

- **Nickname:** His friends and family called him "Ike," and the nickname was used in his popular presidential campaign slogan, "I Like Ike."
- **Interstate System:** President Eisenhower was instrumental in creating the U.S. Interstate Highway System, one of the largest public works projects in American history.
- **NASA:** During his presidency, he signed the act that created NASA, setting the stage for the Space Race with the Soviet Union.
- **Eisenhower Doctrine:** He established the Eisenhower Doctrine, promising military or economic aid to any Middle Eastern country needing help in resisting communist aggression.
- **First Televised Presidential Address:** Eisenhower was the first president to deliver a televised address from the Oval Office, a practice that continues today.
- **President of Columbia University:** Before his presidency, Eisenhower served as the president of Columbia University from 1948 to 1953.
- **Atoms for Peace:** He delivered the "Atoms for Peace" speech to the UN General Assembly, emphasizing the need to use nuclear power for peaceful purposes.
- **Farm Background:** Despite his military and political fame, Eisenhower came from humble beginnings, growing up on a farm in Kansas.

Elizabeth I (Ruler)

- **Virgin Queen:** Elizabeth I is often referred to as the "Virgin Queen" because she never married or had children, keeping the attention on her rule and nation.

- **Golden Age:** Her reign is known as the Elizabethan Era or the "Golden Age," a period of relative peace, prosperity, and the flourishing of the arts, particularly drama and poetry.
- **Language Mastery:** Elizabeth was an accomplished linguist, fluent in six languages: English, Latin, French, Italian, Greek, and Spanish.
- **Survival:** Before becoming queen, Elizabeth was imprisoned by her sister Queen Mary, who saw her as a threat to her throne. Elizabeth survived and later ascended to the throne herself.
- **Shakespeare's Queen:** Some of the most famous works of William Shakespeare were written during the reign of Elizabeth I, often considered a heyday of English literature.
- **Defeat of the Spanish Armada:** Under her command, the English navy famously defeated the Spanish Armada in 1588, marking a significant turning point in English history.
- **Longevity:** Elizabeth I was England's longest reigning Tudor monarch, ruling for 44 years from 1558 to 1603.
- **Education Advocate:** She was a strong supporter of education and was one of the most educated women of her time.
- **Regal Fashion:** Known for her fashion sense, Elizabeth I popularized high forehead hairstyles and white makeup.
- **End of a Dynasty:** She was the last monarch of the House of Tudor, as her death led to the ascension of the House of Stuart with King James I.

Elvis Presley (Singer)

- **King of Rock 'n' Roll:**Known as the "King of Rock 'n' Roll", Elvis Presley is one of the most significant cultural icons of the 20th century.
- **Record Sales:**With estimated record sales of around 600 million units worldwide, Presley is one of the best-selling solo music artists of all time.
- **Musical Influence:**His energized interpretations of songs and sexually provocative performance style, combined with a singularly potent mix of influences, made him enormously popular—and controversial.
- **Nickname:**His dynamic and good-looking presence earned him the nickname "Elvis the Pelvis", much to the dismay of his conservative, middle-aged audience.
- **Film Career:**Besides his music, Presley also had a successful career in films, starring in 31 feature films and two theatrically released concert documentaries.
- **Graceland:**Presley's mansion in Memphis, Tennessee, known as Graceland, is a pilgrimage site for fans and has been designated a National Historic Landmark.
- **Military Service:**At the height of his fame, Presley was drafted into the U.S. Army. His decision to serve in the military, despite his fame, earned him respect from many.
- **Comeback Special:**His '68 Comeback Special on television revived his career, leading to an extended Las Vegas concert residency and a string of profitable tours.
- **First Concert via Satellite:**In 1973, Presley's concert, "Aloha from Hawaii", was the first global broadcast of a concert via satellite and was viewed by approximately 1.5 billion people worldwide.
- **Enduring Legacy:**Despite his untimely death at age 42, Presley's popularity endures, with his music

continuously reissued and remixed, keeping his legacy alive.

Emperor Nero (Ruler)

- **Youthful Ascension:** Nero became the Emperor of Rome at the age of just 17, making him one of the youngest rulers in Roman history.
- **Artistic Ambitions:** Unusually for a Roman emperor, Nero was known for his passion for the arts, particularly music and theatre, often participating in public performances himself.
- **Great Fire of Rome:** Nero famously played the fiddle while Rome burned during the Great Fire in 64 AD, according to legend, though the historical accuracy of this is debated.
- **Christian Persecutions:** Nero is often identified as the first Roman emperor to systematically persecute Christians, blaming them for the Great Fire of Rome.
- **Nero's Golden House:** Following the Great Fire, Nero built an opulent palace complex known as the "Domus Aurea" or "Golden House," which included a colossal statue of himself, the "Colossus of Nero."
- **Revolt and Abandonment:** The widespread discontent with Nero's rule led to the revolt of several Roman provinces in 68 AD, and his subsequent abandonment by the Praetorian Guard.
- **Unusual End:** Nero ended his life by committing suicide after being declared a public enemy by the Senate, reportedly uttering "What an artist dies in me!".

- **Neronian Architecture:**Despite his ill-repute, Nero contributed to Rome's architectural grandeur, building various public buildings, theatres, and aqueducts.
- **Antichrist Allegations:**Some interpretations of the Book of Revelation in the New Testament identify Nero as the Antichrist.
- **Posthumous Rumors:**After Nero's death, many Romans believed in the so-called "Nero Redivivus" legend, expecting that he had not died and would return to reclaim his throne.

Ernest Hemingway (Writer)

- **Literary Giant:**Ernest Hemingway was an American novelist and short-story writer, considered one of the greatest literary figures of the 20th century.
- **Iceberg Theory:**He was known for his distinctive writing style, termed the 'Iceberg Theory', which involved simple, direct prose while implying deeper, underlying themes.
- **War Reporter:**Hemingway served as a war correspondent during five different wars, including World War II and the Spanish Civil War, which significantly influenced his works.
- **Nobel Laureate:**He was awarded the Nobel Prize in Literature in 1954 "for his mastery of the art of narrative, most recently demonstrated in 'The Old Man and the Sea,' and for the influence he has exerted on contemporary style."
- **Adventurous Spirit:**Hemingway was known for his adventurous lifestyle; he was an avid hunter,

fisherman, and bullfighting enthusiast, themes that are often reflected in his works.
- **Tragic End:** Hemingway's life ended tragically when he committed suicide in 1961, following a long battle with depression and physical ailments.
- **Lost Manuscripts:** Hemingway once lost a suitcase containing all his manuscripts for his novels at a train station in Paris, a setback which devastated him.
- **Six-Toed Cats:** Hemingway's home in Key West, now a museum, is known for its population of polydactyl (six-toed) cats, descendants of Hemingway's own pet cat, Snow White.
- **World Record:** In 1938, Hemingway established a world record by catching seven marlin in one day.
- **Surviving Crashes:** Hemingway survived two successive plane crashes while on a safari trip in Africa; he was reported dead in the press, only to resurface alive and with more fantastic tales of his adventures.

Eva Perón (Politician)

- **Humble Origins:** Eva Perón was born into a poor family in rural Argentina and rose to become the First Lady of the country, a testament to her determination and resilience.
- **Stage Beginnings:** Before her political career, Eva Perón was a successful actress in Argentine radio dramas.
- **Iconic First Lady:** Known as "Evita" by the public, she was Argentina's First Lady from 1946 to 1952 and was

immensely popular, especially among the country's working class.
- **Charitable Foundation:** Evita established the Eva Perón Foundation, which provided healthcare and education services for the poor and even built entire communities.
- **Women's Suffrage:** A strong advocate for women's rights, Evita played a key role in achieving women's suffrage in Argentina in 1947.
- **Rainbow Tour:** Her 1947 "Rainbow Tour" of Europe was a significant diplomatic mission, during which she met with leaders like Francisco Franco and Pope Pius XII.
- **Vice Presidency Bid:** In 1951, there was a massive rally to support her nomination for the Vice Presidency, but she declined due to declining health and opposition from the military.
- **Cancer Battle:** Evita died at the young age of 33 from cervical cancer, a fact that was kept secret from her until close to her death.
- **Cult of Personality:** After her death, Evita became a figure of worship, with many seeing her as a saint-like figure for the poor and oppressed.
- **Broadway Star:** Evita's life was turned into the musical "Evita" by Andrew Lloyd Webber and Tim Rice, which became a worldwide sensation and was later adapted into a movie starring Madonna.

Ferdinand Magellan (Explorer)

- **Groundbreaking Journey:** Ferdinand Magellan is best known for leading the first expedition to circumnavigate

the globe, a truly astonishing feat in the early 16th century.
- **Name Legacy:**The Strait of Magellan, a navigable sea route separating mainland South America to the north and Tierra del Fuego to the south, was named after him.
- **Spice Islands:**Magellan's expedition was initially aimed at finding a western route to the Spice Islands, also known as the Maluku Islands in modern-day Indonesia.
- **Portuguese-Born, Spanish-Backed:**Although born in Portugal, it was the Spanish crown that sponsored his voyage around the world.
- **Incomplete Personal Journey:**Despite his expedition's success in circumnavigating the globe, Magellan himself did not complete the journey, as he was killed in the Philippines.
- **Navigational Marvel:**The expedition proved that the world was round and much larger than previously thought, forever changing navigation and exploration.
- **Pacific Naming:**Magellan is credited with naming the Pacific Ocean, deriving the name from the Latin word 'pacificus' meaning peaceful.
- **Interacting with Natives:**His expedition marked the first European contact with the indigenous people of the Marianas and the Philippines.
- **Ship Success:**Only one of the five ships, the Victoria, managed to return to Spain, thus completing the circumnavigation.
- **Intrepid Spirit:**Magellan's journey was one of the greatest exploratory voyages in history and showcased the audacious spirit of human exploration.

Francis Bacon (Philosopher)

- **Scientific Method Proponent:** Francis Bacon is known as the father of empiricism and an early advocate of what would become the scientific method.
- **Royal Counselor:** Bacon held a number of significant posts in the English government, including being appointed Lord Chancellor by King James I.
- **Tainted Reputation:** Despite his brilliance, Bacon's career ended in disgrace as he was charged with 23 counts of corruption and banned from holding office in the kingdom.
- **Writings of Influence:** His philosophical work "Novum Organum" is considered one of the seminal texts in scientific methodology, criticizing the methods of the ancient philosophers and proposing a new approach based on empirical study.
- **Essays Pioneer:** Bacon is also remembered for popularizing the essay as a literary genre with his collection "Essays", which delved into themes ranging from love and truth to death and adversity.
- **Intellectual Diversity:** In addition to philosophy, Bacon wrote on a broad range of subjects, from science and law to history and politics.
- **Baconian Cipher:** He is speculated to have developed a method of secret communication, known as the 'Baconian cipher', based on a binary system.
- **Shakespearean Theory:** A fringe theory suggests that Bacon may have been the true author of William Shakespeare's plays, though this lacks substantial evidence.

- **Mystery Death:**His death was caused by pneumonia, allegedly contracted while studying the effects of freezing on the preservation of meat.
- **Delayed Recognition:**Despite his significant contributions, Bacon's influence on the fields of science and philosophy was not fully recognized until after his death.

Frank Lloyd Wright (Architect)

- **Prolific Creator:**Frank Lloyd Wright designed more than 1,000 structures during his lifetime, more than 500 of which were completed.
- **Prairie Style:**He pioneered the "Prairie School" style of architecture, characterized by low, flat lines that aim to blend buildings with their natural surroundings.
- **Fallingwater Fame:**He designed the iconic house known as "Fallingwater" in rural Pennsylvania, widely considered one of the greatest masterpieces of 20th-century architecture.
- **Education Innovator:**Wright established an educational institution known as the Taliesin Fellowship, where apprentices could learn architecture by working directly on projects.
- **Japanese Influence:**His fascination with Japanese art and architecture influenced his designs and led to him being commissioned to design the Imperial Hotel in Tokyo.
- **Organic Architecture:**Wright promoted the philosophy of "organic architecture," a harmonious relationship between a building, its occupants, and its environment.

- **Guggenheim Genius:**He designed the Guggenheim Museum in New York City, a spiraling building that was controversial at the time but is now recognized as a modernist triumph.
- **Self-Taught:**Despite a brief stint at the University of Wisconsin-Madison, Wright was largely self-taught, and his designs reflect his unique perspective rather than any specific school of architecture.
- **Late Bloomer:**Many of Wright's most iconic works, including Fallingwater and the Guggenheim, were designed when he was in his 70s and 80s, proving age is just a number.
- **Survivor:**He endured personal tragedies including the death of his mother and a fire at his studio that killed six people, but continued to work and create into his 90s.

Franz Kafka (Writer)

- **Unpublished Works:**Kafka instructed his friend Max Brod to destroy all of his manuscripts after his death, but Brod ignored this request, posthumously publishing Kafka's now-famous works instead.
- **Metamorphosis:**His most famous story, "The Metamorphosis," features a man who wakes up one day to find he's been transformed into a giant insect.
- **Day Job:**Despite being one of the most influential writers of the 20th century, Kafka maintained a day job as a lawyer and insurance officer.
- **Bureaucratic Satire:**Kafka's experiences in the bureaucracy of insurance influenced his writing, often showcasing the absurdity and alienation of modern life.

- **Alienation:**Many of Kafka's works explore themes of alienation, guilt, and existential anxiety, which have since become known as "Kafkaesque."
- **Mysterious Disease:**Kafka suffered from a mysterious illness, likely tuberculosis, which caused him great suffering and influenced his dark and despairing writing style.
- **Languages:**Kafka was a German-speaking Jew living in Prague; he was fluent in Czech and studied French and Italian.
- **Unfinished Novels:**Kafka left three unfinished novels, "The Trial," "The Castle," and "Amerika," which are considered his most important longer works.
- **Posthumous Fame:**Kafka's literary fame came after his death, as he only published a few short stories during his lifetime.
- **Fear of Father:**His complex relationship with his father, a dominant and authoritarian figure, heavily influenced his work, a theme most explicitly seen in his Letter to His Father.

Galileo Galilei (Astronomer)

- **Inquisition:**Galileo was famously put on trial by the Catholic Church for his belief in heliocentrism and was forced to recant his views.
- **Telescope:**Although he did not invent the telescope, Galileo was the first person to use it for astronomical purposes, discovering the moons of Jupiter.
- **Dropped Objects:**Galileo is often associated with the Leaning Tower of Pisa, where he supposedly dropped

two different weighted balls to disprove Aristotle's theory of gravity.
- **Moon Craters:** He was the first person to note that the Moon's surface is not smooth but covered in craters.
- **Star Catalog:** Galileo cataloged the stars and was the first to observe that the Milky Way is made up of stars.
- **Blindness:** Galileo became blind in the last years of his life, likely as a result of long-term exposure to the sun through his telescope.
- **"Eppur si muove":** The phrase "And yet it moves" is attributed to Galileo, allegedly uttered after being forced to deny that the Earth moves around the Sun.
- **Inventions:** Galileo is credited with inventing the thermoscope, an early version of the thermometer.
- **Jupiter's Moons:** Galileo discovered four of Jupiter's largest moons, which are now known as the Galilean moons.
- **Moon Naming:** For a short period, Galileo named the moons of Jupiter after his patron Cosimo II de' Medici, leading to their initial naming as the "Medicean Stars".

George Harrison (Musician)

- **Youngest Beatle:** George Harrison, the lead guitarist of The Beatles, was the youngest member of the band.
- **Eastern Influence:** He was instrumental in introducing Indian classical music and instruments to the Western world, notably the sitar.
- **Concert for Bangladesh:** Harrison organized the Concert for Bangladesh in 1971, which is often considered the first major charity benefit concert.

- **Solo Success:** Post The Beatles, Harrison achieved significant solo success, including his triple album "All Things Must Pass".
- **Traveling Wilburys:** He co-founded the supergroup the Traveling Wilburys with Bob Dylan, Roy Orbison, Tom Petty, and Jeff Lynne in the late 1980s.
- **Movie Producer:** Through his production company, HandMade Films, Harrison produced several British cult classics, including "Monty Python's Life of Brian".
- **Autobiography:** His autobiography, "I, Me, Mine," was published in 1980 and covers his life up to that point in great detail.
- **Posthumous Star:** A star was dedicated to Harrison on the Hollywood Walk of Fame posthumously in 2009.
- **Gardening Passion:** Harrison had a profound love for gardening and spent years restoring the garden of his home, Friar Park.
- **Astral Weeks:** According to Paul McCartney, Harrison's last words were "Love one another," a testament to his lifelong commitment to spiritual growth and unity.

Georgia O'Keeffe (Painter)

- **Modernist Pioneer:** Georgia O'Keeffe is often referred to as the "Mother of American modernism," having been instrumental in introducing abstract art to the United States.
- **Flower Focus:** She is best known for her enlarged, highly detailed paintings of flowers, which some interpret as a feminist reclamation of the traditionally "feminine" subject matter.

- **Inspired by Nature:** Much of her work was inspired by the natural beauty she found in New Mexico, where she lived for much of her life.
- **Price Record:** In 2014, O'Keeffe's painting "Jimson Weed/White Flower No. 1" sold for $44.4 million, setting a record for the highest price for a work by a female artist.
- **Stieglitz Muse:** She had a long romantic and professional relationship with the influential photographer Alfred Stieglitz, who helped launch her career.
- **Black-and-White:** Georgia O'Keeffe was known for wearing mostly black and white, reflecting her minimalist aesthetic.
- **Living Legend:** In 1985, she was awarded the National Medal of Arts, one of the highest honors for an artist in the United States.
- **Her Own Museum:** The Georgia O'Keeffe Museum in Santa Fe, New Mexico, is dedicated to her work and life.
- **Talent Recognition:** She began studying art at a young age and her talent was recognized when she was just 10 years old.
- **Artistic Longevity:** Despite suffering from macular degeneration later in life, which severely impaired her vision, O'Keeffe continued to create art into her 90s using clay and other tactile mediums.

Mahatma Gandhi (Activist)

- **Moniker:** "Mahatma," the name most associated with Gandhi, is not his given name but an honorific title meaning "great soul" in Sanskrit.
- **Lawyer First:** Before becoming a civil rights activist, Gandhi trained and worked as a lawyer in London and South Africa.
- **Salt March:** Gandhi led a 240-mile march to the Arabian Sea to protest the British salt tax, a pivotal event in India's fight for independence.
- **Nonviolent Resistance:** Gandhi developed the concept of "satyagraha," or nonviolent resistance, which greatly influenced civil rights movements worldwide, including the American Civil Rights Movement led by Dr. Martin Luther King Jr.
- **Fasting:** Gandhi frequently used hunger strikes as a form of political protest, and his longest fast lasted 21 days.
- **Assassination:** Despite his commitment to non-violence, Gandhi was assassinated by a Hindu extremist in 1948.
- **Nobel Peace Prize:** Despite being nominated five times, Gandhi never won the Nobel Peace Prize. In 1948, the year of his death, the award was not given, with the committee stating there was "no suitable living candidate."
- **Charkha:** Gandhi's use of the spinning wheel, or charkha, as a symbol of Indian self-sufficiency and resistance to British rule became an iconic image of the independence movement.
- **Simple Living:** Gandhi was renowned for his simple lifestyle. He owned very few possessions and made his own clothes, spinning the cotton himself.

- **Time's Person of the Year:** In 1930, Gandhi was named Time magazine's "Man of the Year", becoming the first non-European to earn this distinction.

Grace Hopper (Computer Scientist)

- **Bug Inventor:** Grace Hopper is credited with popularizing the term "bug" to describe a glitch in a computer system, after an actual moth was found causing problems in a machine.
- **COBOL Pioneer:** Hopper was instrumental in the development of COBOL, one of the first high-level programming languages.
- **Ph.D. Holder:** She earned a Ph.D. in mathematics from Yale University in 1934, an unusual achievement for a woman of her time.
- **Navy Rear Admiral:** She was one of the few women to attain the rank of rear admiral in the U.S. Navy.
- **Longest Serving:** Hopper served in the U.S. Navy for more than 40 years, making her one of the longest-serving women in the armed forces.
- **First Female:** She was the first woman to receive the National Medal of Technology and Innovation, one of the highest honors in the field of technology in the U.S.
- **First Compiler:** She led the team that invented the first compiler, a software program that translates high-level language into machine code.
- **Nanosecond Icon:** Hopper was known for using lengths of wire to visually represent a nanosecond, enhancing her teaching of computing concepts.

- **Late Bloomer:** Despite being a key figure in computing, Hopper didn't actually start working with computers until she was in her late 30s.
- **Google Doodle:** In 2013, Google honored her with a doodle on their homepage, showcasing her work on the computer and the famous 'bug'.

Greta Garbo (Actress)

- **Swedish Star:** Greta Garbo, a Swedish-American actress, was a prominent figure during Hollywood's silent and early talkie eras.
- **Oscar Nominations:** Throughout her career, Garbo was nominated for an Academy Award three times, but she never won the award in competition.
- **Retirement Age:** She retired at the age of 35, after a successful career, and lived the rest of her life in relative seclusion.
- **Talkie Triumph:** Garbo successfully transitioned from silent movies to "talkies," with her first talking film, "Anna Christie," promoted with the tagline "Garbo Talks!"
- **Never Married:** Despite many relationships and engagements, Garbo never married, adding to her mysterious persona.
- **Honorary Award:** Despite never winning in competition, Garbo was given an Honorary Academy Award in 1954 for her "unforgettable screen performances."
- **AFI Recognition:** The American Film Institute ranked Garbo fifth on their list of the greatest female stars of classic Hollywood cinema.

- **On-Screen Introvert:** Garbo's roles often involved complex women of mystery and melancholy, reflecting her own private nature.
- **Philanthropist:** After her retirement, Garbo was a generous but discreet philanthropist, contributing to causes such as animal welfare.
- **Posthumous Recognition:** Garbo was awarded a star on the Hollywood Walk of Fame in 1960, eight years before her death.

Guy Fawkes (Revolutionary)

- **Firestarter:** Guy Fawkes is most famously known for his part in the failed Gunpowder Plot of 1605, where he aimed to blow up England's Houses of Parliament.
- **Catholic Cause:** The motive behind the plot was to end the persecution of Roman Catholics by the English government.
- **A Name Change:** Born as Guido Fawkes in April 1570, he later adopted the Italian version of his name while fighting for the Spanish in the Eighty Years' War.
- **In the Shadows:** Despite being the most recognized figure, Fawkes was not the leader of the Gunpowder Plot but was in charge of executing the plan due to his military experience.
- **Busted Below:** Fawkes was arrested on November 5, 1605, in a cellar beneath the House of Lords where 36 barrels of gunpowder were stored.
- **Torturous Times:** Fawkes was subjected to severe torture following his arrest, which led him to disclose the names of his fellow plotters.

- **Execution Evolution:**Fawkes was sentenced to be hanged, drawn, and quartered, but he leapt from the gallows, breaking his neck, thus avoiding the agony of the full execution.
- **Festival of Fire:**The thwarting of the Gunpowder Plot is celebrated annually in the UK on November 5, known as Guy Fawkes Night, with bonfires and fireworks.
- **Masked Movement:**The Guy Fawkes mask, popularized by the graphic novel and film "V for Vendetta," has become a universal symbol for anti-establishment protests.
- **Spectacular Symbol:**Though seen as a traitor in his lifetime, Guy Fawkes has transformed into a symbol of rebellion and resistance, showing how historical figures can be reinterpreted over time.

H.P. Lovecraft (Writer)

- **Cosmic Horror:**Lovecraft is famous for creating a unique genre of fiction, "Lovecraftian horror", which emphasizes cosmic horror of the unknown and the insignificant role of humanity in the universe's much larger scheme.
- **Cthulhu Mythos:**Lovecraft's best-known works form part of what's later been termed the "Cthulhu Mythos," a shared universe used by other authors in a variety of media, expanding on Lovecraft's themes and settings.
- **Unappreciated in Life:**Despite his posthumous fame, Lovecraft's work was virtually unknown during his lifetime, and he struggled with poverty.

- **Epistolary Virtuoso:** Lovecraft was a prolific letter writer, with estimates suggesting he wrote over 100,000 letters in his lifetime.
- **Self-taught:** Lovecraft was mostly self-educated, having left school after experiencing a nervous breakdown at the age of eight.
- **Astronomical Ambitions:** As a teenager, Lovecraft wanted to be an astronomer, but his lack of mathematical knowledge prevented him from doing so.
- **Fear of Seafood:** Despite creating various ocean-dwelling monsters, Lovecraft had a strong dislike for seafood and found it revolting.
- **Never Left Home:** Lovecraft had a fear of traveling and spent most of his life in his home state of Rhode Island.
- **Alien Architecture:** In his writings, Lovecraft frequently used non-Euclidean geometry, a mathematical concept that bends the laws of physics, to describe the alien nature of his otherworldly entities and locations.
- **Undying Influence:** His work has inspired a wide range of writers, musicians, and filmmakers, including Stephen King, Neil Gaiman, and Guillermo del Toro, proving his legacy in the realm of horror and fantasy.

Harriet Tubman (Abolitionist)

- **Escape Artist:** Harriet Tubman escaped slavery and subsequently made about 13 rescue missions to rescue approximately 70 enslaved people using the Underground Railroad.

- **Nickname:** She was nicknamed "Moses" after the biblical figure who led the Hebrews to freedom from Egypt, due to her role in leading slaves to freedom.
- **Spying:** During the Civil War, Tubman worked for the Union Army as a cook, nurse, armed scout, and spy.
- **Successful Raid:** She was the first woman to lead an armed expedition in the Civil War and guided the raid at Combahee Ferry, which liberated more than 700 slaves.
- **Injury Impact:** Tubman suffered a head injury as a child that caused her to experience visions and dreams she interpreted as revelations from God. These visions would frequently incapacitate her, but she considered them a guiding force in her life.
- **Suffragist:** After the Civil War, Tubman was active in the women's suffrage movement, working alongside figures like Susan B. Anthony and Elizabeth Cady Stanton.
- **Honoring her Work:** In 2016, the U.S. Treasury Department announced that Tubman would replace Andrew Jackson on the center of a new $20 bill, making her the first African American woman to appear on U.S. currency.
- **Personal Sacrifices:** Despite her heroism and contributions, Tubman lived in poverty for most of her life, often giving away what little she had to others in need.
- **Home for Elderly:** She opened the Harriet Tubman Home for the Aged on a property adjacent to her own residence to support elderly African Americans, showing her dedication to humanitarian causes.
- **An Act of Bravery:** Tubman's daring rescues and tireless advocacy were a testament to her indomitable

spirit. Her life remains a powerful symbol of the fight against slavery and injustice.

Harry S. Truman (Politician)

- **Middle Name:** The "S" in Harry S. Truman doesn't stand for anything; it was given to honor both of his grandfathers, Anderson Shipp Truman and Solomon Young.
- **Unexpected Presidency:** Truman assumed the presidency on April 12, 1945, when President Roosevelt died less than three months into his fourth term.
- **Atomic Decision:** Truman made the controversial decision to drop atomic bombs on Hiroshima and Nagasaki in Japan to hasten the end of World War II.
- **Marshalling Plan:** Under Truman's leadership, the Marshall Plan was launched, providing more than $13 billion (over $130 billion today) to help Europe recover from the devastation of World War II.
- **Historic Election:** Truman won the 1948 presidential election in a major upset against Thomas E. Dewey, despite many polls and newspapers predicting his defeat.
- **Desk Sign:** Truman was known for a sign on his desk that read "The Buck Stops Here", emphasizing his belief in taking responsibility for all decisions made in his administration.
- **Music Love:** Truman was a talented pianist and often played in his spare time. He once said, "If I could have been, I would rather have been a great pianist."
- **Korean War:** Truman was the president during the start of the Korean War, and his decision to enter the

conflict marked a crucial moment in the early days of the Cold War.
- **Integrated Military:**Truman issued Executive Order 9981 in 1948, which led to the desegregation of the United States military.
- **Personal Letters:**Throughout his life, Truman wrote long, insightful letters to his wife, Bess, revealing his thoughts on everything from his love for her to his presidential decisions. These letters are now treasured historical documents.

Helen Keller (Author)

- **Sensory Loss:**Helen Keller, at the age of 19 months, became both blind and deaf due to an illness, possibly scarlet fever or meningitis.
- **Language Breakthrough:**The word "water" was Keller's breakthrough in communication, spelled into her hand by her teacher, Anne Sullivan, as water flowed over her other hand.
- **Radcliffe Graduate:**Despite her challenges, Keller graduated with honors from Radcliffe College in 1904, becoming the first deaf-blind person to earn a Bachelor of Arts degree.
- **Author:**She authored numerous books and essays, including "The Story of My Life," which has been translated into over 50 languages.
- **Advocate:**Keller was a prominent advocate for people with disabilities, women's suffrage, and worker's rights.

- **Akita Dog:** She is credited with introducing the Akita breed of dog to America after being gifted one by the Japanese government.
- **Vaudeville Career:** During the 1920s, Keller even embarked on a brief vaudeville career to earn money.
- **Presidential Medal:** In 1964, President Lyndon B. Johnson awarded her the Presidential Medal of Freedom, one of the United States' highest civilian honors.
- **Meeting Every US President:** From Grover Cleveland to Lyndon B. Johnson, Keller met every US President in office during her lifetime.
- **Long Friendship:** Helen's relationship with her teacher, Anne Sullivan, lasted 49 years, until Sullivan's death in 1936.

Henry VIII (Ruler)

- **Multiple Marriages:** Henry VIII is famously known for his six marriages, two of which ended in the execution of his wives, Anne Boleyn and Catherine Howard.
- **Break with Rome:** He broke England's ties with the Roman Catholic Church to form the Church of England, primarily to annul his first marriage and remarry, changing the religious landscape of England forever.
- **Legitimate Heirs:** Despite his many marriages, only three of Henry VIII's children survived infancy and are recognized as legitimate heirs: Mary I, Elizabeth I, and Edward VI.
- **Musical Monarch:** Henry was an accomplished musician, author, and poet; some of his compositions are still performed today.

- **Obesity:**Henry VIII was athletic and slender in his youth, but later in life, he became obese due to a jousting injury that left him largely immobile and led to his early death at 55.
- **Warrior King:**He was a keen military leader, known for launching ambitious and costly wars against France and Scotland.
- **Royal Navy:**Henry VIII is known as the 'Father of the English navy'; he expanded the naval fleet from just a few ships to over 50.
- **Relics:**He ordered the destruction of shrines to saints and the seizure of church lands, resulting in the displacement of thousands of monks and nuns.
- **Surviving Armor:**The armor of Henry VIII, showcased in the Tower of London, is one of the best surviving examples of 16th-century military fashion.
- **Rhyme Reminder:**The fates of his six wives are commonly remembered with a rhyme: "Divorced, beheaded, died; divorced, beheaded, survived."

Hippocrates (Physician)

- **Foundation:**Known as the "Father of Medicine", Hippocrates fundamentally transformed the practice of medicine in ancient Greece.
- **Hippocratic Oath:**He is credited with the creation of the Hippocratic Oath, an ethical code still used by physicians today.
- **Diagnostic Approach:**Hippocrates is celebrated for his systematic approach to diagnosing diseases based on symptoms and physical examinations rather than superstitions.

- **Ancient Texts:** He authored a body of medical texts known as the 'Hippocratic Corpus', although not all these works can be definitively attributed to him.
- **Four Humors:** Hippocrates was the proponent of the theory of the 'Four Humors', suggesting that the body contained four basic substances: blood, black bile, yellow bile, and phlegm.
- **Disease Theory:** He was among the first to believe that diseases were caused naturally, not because of superstition or gods.
- **Case Histories:** Hippocrates often recorded detailed observations of many medical conditions, making him one of the first to document case histories.
- **Preventive Medicine:** Hippocrates emphasized diet and exercise as key factors in health, laying early groundwork for the concept of preventive medicine.
- **Brain Function:** He was one of the first to recognize the brain as the center of thought, intelligence, and emotion.
- **Longevity:** Despite the vast advances in medical knowledge since his time, Hippocrates's emphasis on holistic and rational treatment continues to influence medical practice to this day.

Hubert de Givenchy (Fashion Designer)

- **Fashion Icon:** Hubert de Givenchy was a renowned French fashion designer who founded the house of Givenchy in 1952.
- **Audrey Hepburn's Designer:** Givenchy is perhaps best known for his close relationship with actress Audrey Hepburn, for whom he designed many iconic

costumes, including her little black dress in 'Breakfast at Tiffany's'.
- **The Bettina Blouse:**Givenchy's first collection featured the "Bettina Blouse," named after Bettina Graziani, France's leading model at the time, which achieved instant fame.
- **New Standards:**He was praised for his modern and innovative designs that helped to redefine standards of elegance in the fashion world.
- **Separates Concept:**Givenchy introduced the concept of "separates" - blouses and skirts, which offered women a range of mix-and-match possibilities.
- **Luxury Perfumes:**The Givenchy brand is also famous for its line of luxury perfumes, with the first fragrance, L'Interdit, originally created for Audrey Hepburn.
- **Royal Clientele:**Givenchy's clientele included many royal and famous figures, including the Duchess of Windsor, Jackie Kennedy, and Princess Grace of Monaco.
- **Retirement:**After a brilliant career, Givenchy retired in 1995 and his fashion house was subsequently led by several famous designers, including Alexander McQueen and Riccardo Tisci.
- **Minimalist Aesthetic:**Givenchy was admired for his minimalist, chic designs that elegantly combined simplicity with high-quality craftsmanship.
- **Honoring Givenchy:**In 2018, the fashion world mourned Givenchy's passing and celebrated his contributions to the industry, including his emphasis on empowering women through fashion.

Isaac Asimov (Writer)

- **Multi-genre Mastery:** Isaac Asimov was a highly prolific writer, penning over 500 books that covered a broad range of topics, from science fiction and mysteries to non-fiction works on mathematics, history, and science.
- **Three Laws of Robotics:** Asimov introduced the now-famous "Three Laws of Robotics" in his 1942 short story "Runaround," a concept that has significantly influenced science fiction and the philosophical discussion about artificial intelligence.
- **Foundation Series:** Asimov's "Foundation" series is considered one of the greatest achievements in science fiction literature, with a narrative that spans thousands of years and a complex, multi-generational cast of characters.
- **Biochemistry Background:** Apart from his writing career, Asimov was a trained biochemist with a Ph.D. from Columbia University, and he worked as an associate professor of biochemistry at Boston University School of Medicine.
- **Good Behavior Ribbon:** As a serviceman in World War II, Asimov received a "Good Behavior Ribbon" but humorously noted that it was issued by default as they didn't have a "Bad Behavior Ribbon."
- **Writing Speed:** Asimov was known for his extraordinary writing speed, often producing an average of 5,000 words a day, and attributed his productivity to a disciplined schedule and a lack of writer's block.
- **Science Popularizer:** He made significant contributions to the public understanding of science, writing popular science books that explained complex topics in an accessible way.

- **Prolific Essayist:** Asimov wrote a science column for "The Magazine of Fantasy and Science Fiction" for 33 years, never missing a single issue.
- **Robot Series:** His "Robot" series, featuring the detective Elijah Baley and the humanoid robot R. Daneel Olivaw, combined elements of the detective genre with science fiction, creating a unique blend.
- **Asimov's Predictions:** Asimov made a number of future predictions in his writings, some of which have been remarkably accurate, including ideas about automation, artificial intelligence, and digital learning.

Ivan the Terrible (Ruler)

- **First Tsar:** Ivan IV, known as Ivan the Terrible, was the first ruler of Russia to assume the title of Tsar, a term that can be translated as 'Emperor'.
- **Child King:** Ivan became Grand Prince of Moscow at the age of three after his father's death, marking the beginning of a complex and tumultuous reign.
- **Killer Tsar:** Ivan's reputation for violence includes an incident where he killed his own son, Ivan Ivanovich, in a fit of rage, leaving Russia without a competent heir.
- **Mental Health:** It's speculated that Ivan suffered from mental illness, which may have contributed to his erratic and often cruel behavior.
- **Expansionist:** Ivan expanded the Russian empire significantly, laying the groundwork for it to become a major European power.
- **Architectural Legacy:** He commissioned the building of the iconic St. Basil's Cathedral in Moscow's Red Square, a symbol of Russia to this day.

- **Nickname:** The term "Terrible" in Ivan's moniker doesn't mean "horrible", but rather it refers to the old English usage of "causing terror" as in "inspiring fear".
- **Literacy:** Despite his reputation, Ivan was highly intelligent, known for his interest in theology and his ability to speak several languages.
- **Print Pioneer:** He established the first printing press in Russia, bringing a new level of literacy and knowledge dissemination to his kingdom.
- **Oprichnina:** Ivan created a policy known as the Oprichnina, where he seized lands and instilled a reign of terror to maintain control, which led to the massacre of Novgorod.

Jackie Robinson (Baseball Player)

- **Barrier Breaker:** Jackie Robinson famously broke the color barrier in Major League Baseball (MLB) when he debuted with the Brooklyn Dodgers in 1947.
- **Rookie of the Year:** In his first year, Robinson won the inaugural MLB Rookie of the Year Award.
- **Military Service:** Before his baseball career, Robinson served as a second lieutenant in the United States Army during World War II, but never saw combat due to racial segregation policies.
- **Civil Rights Activist:** Outside of baseball, Robinson was a prominent civil rights activist, using his platform to fight racial inequality.
- **Multi-Sport Athlete:** Robinson was an exceptional multi-sport athlete at UCLA, playing football, basketball, track, and baseball.

- **Hall of Famer:** He was inducted into the Baseball Hall of Fame in 1962, his first year of eligibility.
- **Retired Number:** Robinson's jersey number, 42, was universally retired across all MLB teams in 1997, a first in the history of the league.
- **Post-Baseball Career:** After retiring from baseball, Robinson became a successful businessman and the first Black television analyst in MLB.
- **Congressional Gold Medal:** Posthumously, in 2005, he was awarded the Congressional Gold Medal, the highest civilian award in the United States.
- **Jackie Robinson Day:** Every April 15th, MLB celebrates Jackie Robinson Day, where every player on every team wears number 42 in his honor.

James Dean (Actor)

- **Super Star Status:** James Dean, despite having a brief career and starring in only three major films, became a cultural icon of teenage disillusionment and rebellion.
- **Posthumous Praise:** He is the only actor to have received two posthumous Academy Award nominations, for "East of Eden" (1955) and "Giant" (1956).
- **Lifelong Love:** Dean developed a love for car racing and purchased several vehicles, including the Porsche Spyder in which he met his tragic end.
- **Tragic Triumph:** His last film "Giant" was still in post-production when he died; it went on to earn ten Academy Award nominations.

- **Screen Test Start:**Dean began his acting career with a Pepsi commercial and several uncredited roles in films and TV shows.
- **Broadway Bound:**Before his film career, Dean was a successful stage actor and won the "Theatre World Award" for his role in "See the Jaguar".
- **Rebellious Role:**His role as Jim Stark in "Rebel Without a Cause" (1955) made him a symbol of youth rebellion, and the red jacket he wore in the film became a fashion staple.
- **Admiration for the Arts:**Besides acting, Dean was also interested in painting, sculpture, and photography.
- **Quirky Fact:**Dean was ambidextrous, which allowed him to write and draw with both hands.
- **Legends Never Die:**Even decades after his untimely death, Dean remains a symbol of youthful rebellion and continues to inspire countless biographies, documentaries, and films.

Janis Joplin (Singer)

- **Psychedelic Performer:**Known as "The Queen of Psychedelic Soul," Janis Joplin was a pioneering figure in the counterculture movement of the 1960s.
- **Vocal Vortex:**Joplin's raw and powerful mezzo-soprano voice helped her stand out in the male-dominated rock music scene of her era.
- **Festival Fame:**Her performance at the Woodstock Music Festival in 1969 skyrocketed her to international fame, solidifying her status as a music icon.

- **Posthumous Praise:** Her album "Pearl" was released posthumously and topped the Billboard 200, featuring her number one hit, "Me and Bobby McGee."
- **Iconic Influence:** Janis Joplin is often cited as a major influence by many successful female rock artists, including Stevie Nicks and Pink.
- **Texas Tribute:** A life-size bronze statue of Joplin has been erected in her hometown of Port Arthur, Texas, as a tribute to her significant impact on music.
- **Brief Brilliance:** Joplin's mainstream career was tragically short, spanning only four years before her untimely death at the age of 27 due to a heroin overdose.
- **Rock and Roll Royalty:** She was posthumously inducted into the Rock and Roll Hall of Fame in 1995, cementing her legacy in the music world.
- **Expressive Ensemble:** Known for her flamboyant outfits, Joplin's personal style with feathers, beads, and bell-bottoms became a symbol of the '60s counterculture.
- **Biographical Broadway:** "A Night with Janis Joplin," a Broadway musical celebrating Joplin and her biggest musical influences, was nominated for a Tony Award in 2014.

Jim Henson (Puppeteer)

- **Muppet Mastermind:** Jim Henson is most famously known as the creator of The Muppets, a cast of puppet characters that became iconic in American television and film.

- **Primetime Puppetry:**Henson brought puppetry to primetime television through his innovative variety show, "The Muppet Show," which attracted adult audiences and won numerous awards, including three Primetime Emmy Awards.
- **Sesame Street Success:**Henson played a critical role in the early development of "Sesame Street," creating characters like Big Bird, Oscar the Grouch, and the beloved Kermit the Frog.
- **Fantasy Films:**Besides his puppetry work, Henson directed the fantasy films "The Dark Crystal" and "Labyrinth," showcasing his knack for storytelling and creative puppetry.
- **Green Guy:**The prototype of Henson's most famous character, Kermit the Frog, was made from his mother's old spring coat and two halves of a ping-pong ball.
- **First Steps:**Henson's career started when he was still a high school student with a five-minute puppet show called "Sam and Friends," which aired twice daily on a local Washington D.C. television station.
- **Distinctive Voice:**Henson not only created the Muppets but also performed many of their voices, including Kermit the Frog, Rowlf the Dog, and Dr. Teeth.
- **Untimely Death:**Henson's sudden death in 1990 from a rare streptococcal infection led to a wave of public mourning and posthumous accolades, including the renaming of a stretch of New York City's 67th Street as "Jim Henson's Muppet Place."
- **Education Enthusiast:**A firm believer in the educational power of television, Henson used "Sesame

Street" to teach children fundamental lessons about numbers, letters, and social interaction.
- **Creature Creation:** Henson established Jim Henson's Creature Shop, one of the world's leading puppet-building, animatronics, and digital visual effects workshops, which has contributed to films like "The NeverEnding Story," "Harry Potter," and "The Hitchhiker's Guide to the Galaxy."

Joan of Arc (Military Leader)

- **Divine Voices:** Joan of Arc, known as the "Maid of Orléans," claimed to have been guided by voices from saints since her early teen years, directing her to aid the Dauphin (future King Charles VII) in the Hundred Years' War against England.
- **Armor-clad Warrior:** Despite being a peasant girl, Joan of Arc rose to lead the French army into several important victories, most notably the siege of Orléans, always dressed in a suit of white armor.
- **No Training:** Joan never received any formal military training, yet was able to plan and execute tactical maneuvers that led to significant French victories.
- **Heretic Trial:** Captured by the English allies, Joan was put on trial for heresy and witchcraft, based largely on her claims of divine guidance and her unconventional choice to wear male military attire.
- **Martyrdom:** Joan of Arc was burned at the stake in Rouen, France, in 1431, at the age of 19, cementing her status as a martyr.
- **Posthumous Pardon:** In 1456, Joan was posthumously retried and found innocent by the Catholic Church, 25 years after her execution.

- **Canonization:** Joan of Arc was canonized as a saint by the Catholic Church in 1920, nearly 500 years after her death.
- **Icon of France:** Joan of Arc is one of the patron saints of France and is considered a national heroine, with her image used to represent French patriotism and resistance.
- **Illiteracy:** Despite leading armies and meeting with nobility, Joan was illiterate; she relied on others to write her dictated letters.
- **Influence on Literature:** Joan's dramatic life story has been the subject of countless books, plays, and films, including George Bernard Shaw's "Saint Joan" and Mark Twain's "Personal Recollections of Joan of Arc."

Johannes Kepler (Astronomer)

- **Laws of Planetary Motion:** Kepler is famous for formulating three laws of planetary motion that accurately describe the movements of planets around the Sun.
- **Mathematical Brilliance:** Despite being frequently sick and having poor vision, Kepler excelled in mathematics and eventually became a key figure in the 17th-century scientific revolution.
- **Supernova Sightings:** Kepler observed a supernova in 1604, writing a book about the event, which is now known as Kepler's Supernova.
- **Mars Observations:** Kepler's detailed observations and mathematical analysis of Mars were instrumental in formulating his laws of planetary motion.

- **Astrology Adherence:** Interestingly, despite his scientific rigor, Kepler also believed in astrology and often cast horoscopes to supplement his income.
- **Defending His Mother:** Kepler's mother, Katharina, was accused of witchcraft, and Kepler took a break from his work to successfully defend her in the court.
- **Science Fiction Pioneer:** Kepler wrote the first work of science fiction, "Somnium", which presented a detailed imaginative description of how the Earth might look from the Moon.
- **Troubled Times:** Kepler lived through a time of religious wars in Europe, and his Protestant faith caused him to lose his job when his region was taken over by Catholic forces.
- **Refining The Telescope:** Kepler improved the design of the refracting telescope by using a convex lens for the eyepiece instead of Galileo's concave one, improving the field of view.
- **Unmarked Grave:** Despite his monumental contributions, Kepler was buried in an unmarked grave after his death in 1630 – a casualty of the Thirty Years War.

John Locke (Philosopher)

- **Empiricism Advocate:** John Locke is widely known as the "Father of Empiricism," promoting the idea that knowledge comes primarily from sensory experience.
- **Tabula Rasa:** He championed the concept of 'Tabula Rasa' or 'blank slate,' suggesting that we are born without built-in mental content, and all our knowledge comes from experience or perception.

- **Influential Works:** His seminal work "Two Treatises of Government" significantly influenced political philosophy and provided a foundation for liberal democratic ideas.
- **Early Life:** Despite becoming a significant philosopher, Locke initially studied medicine at Oxford University and practiced as a doctor.
- **Political Activism:** Locke was deeply involved in English politics and had a strong influence on the Whig party's ideology.
- **Education Views:** He wrote extensively on education and believed that it should focus on the development of the mind rather than rote memorization.
- **Religious Tolerance:** In a time of religious persecution, Locke advocated for religious tolerance and believed that governments should not have control over individuals' religious beliefs.
- **American Revolution:** Locke's philosophy heavily influenced the American Revolution, with his ideas on life, liberty, and property echoing in the United States Declaration of Independence.
- **Medical Innovations:** Beyond his philosophical pursuits, Locke made contributions to medicine and was credited with the discovery of the medical use of nitrous oxide.
- **Posthumous Influence:** Although his ideas were not universally accepted during his lifetime, Locke's influence grew after his death, and his works continue to be studied by scholars around the world.

Joseph Stalin (Politician)

- **The Man of Steel:** Joseph Stalin's real name was Ioseb Besarionis dze Jughashvili; he adopted 'Stalin', meaning 'man of steel' in Russian, as his revolutionary pseudonym.
- **Master Planner:** Stalin oversaw and implemented a series of Five-Year Plans starting from 1928, which aimed at industrializing the Soviet Union rapidly, but it also led to the starvation and death of millions.
- **Massive Purges:** As part of his iron-fisted rule, Stalin conducted the Great Purge from 1936 to 1938, in which millions of people, including top-ranking military officials and party members, were arrested, executed, or sent to labor camps.
- **WWII Leadership:** Stalin led the USSR through the devastating hardships of World War II, which saw about 26 million Soviet citizens lose their lives, but eventually ended with the defeat of Nazi Germany.
- **Time's Person:** Despite his reputation as a ruthless leader, Stalin was named Time magazine's Person of the Year twice, in 1939 and 1942.
- **Secret Passion:** Unknown to many, Stalin had a passion for cinema and used to personally review every film made in the USSR.
- **Cult of Personality:** Stalin established a powerful cult of personality around himself, which portrayed him as a caring leader and father of the nation, despite his tyrannical rule.
- **Poetry Affection:** Before becoming a political figure, young Stalin had several of his poems published in Georgian newspapers, showing his literary inclination.
- **Children's Fate:** Stalin's son Yakov was captured by the Nazis during WWII, and when the Germans

proposed a prisoner exchange, Stalin reportedly said, "I have no son named Yakov."
- **Iron Curtain:**Stalin's policies and ideologies, especially his establishment of Communist governments in Eastern Europe post-WWII, led to the creation of the 'Iron Curtain', eventually leading to the Cold War.

Julia Child (Chef)

- **Spy Beginnings:**Before becoming a renowned chef, Julia Child worked for the Office of Strategic Services (OSS), the precursor to the CIA, during World War II.
- **Late Starter:**Julia Child didn't start cooking until she was in her 30s, proving it's never too late to pursue your passion.
- **French Cuisine Pioneer:**Child is credited with bringing French cuisine to the American public with her debut cookbook "Mastering the Art of French Cooking".
- **TV Icon:**Her television show "The French Chef" was one of the first cooking shows on American television and made her a household name.
- **Kitchen Collection:**Julia Child's kitchen, which she referred to as her "magic set", is on display at the Smithsonian's National Museum of American History.
- **Gigantic Personality:**Standing at an impressive 6'2", Child was known for her distinctive and enthusiastic voice that captivated audiences on her TV shows.
- **Egg Enthusiast:**She reportedly used 573 eggs in the process of writing and testing the recipe for her acclaimed French dessert, "Queen of Sheba" chocolate cake.

- **White House Dinner:** Julia Child once cooked for a state dinner at the White House during President Jimmy Carter's term.
- **Presidential Honor:** In 2003, Child was awarded the Presidential Medal of Freedom by President George W. Bush for her contributions to the culinary world.
- **Spunky Spirit:** Child was known for her lively personality and quick wit, once famously quipping, "The only time to eat diet food is while you're waiting for the steak to cook".

Katharine Hepburn (Actress)

- **Record Holder:** Katharine Hepburn holds the record for the most Best Actress Academy Awards won, with a total of four wins.
- **Rebel:** Hepburn was known for her rebellious nature, including her refusal to conform to Hollywood's beauty standards by often wearing pants, which was considered unorthodox for women at the time.
- **Stuntwoman:** She did many of her own stunts in her movies, including back flips, high dives, and horse-riding.
- **Shakespearean Actress:** Hepburn also had a notable stage career, performing in various Shakespeare plays including "The Merchant of Venice" and "Much Ado About Nothing."
- **Refusal of Interviews:** Known for her fiercely private nature, Hepburn rarely gave interviews and avoided the Hollywood social scene.

- **Tough Childhood:**Hepburn had to overcome several personal tragedies in her early life, including the suicide of her older brother.
- **Never Attended Oscar Ceremonies:**Despite winning four Oscars, Hepburn never attended an Academy Awards ceremony to accept her awards in person until 1974.
- **Life-Long Romance:**Hepburn was in a 26-year-long relationship with actor Spencer Tracy, but they never married because Tracy, a Catholic, would not divorce his wife.
- **Golf Enthusiast:**She was a passionate golfer and even had a golf course in the yard of her Connecticut home.
- **Longevity:**Hepburn enjoyed a career that spanned over six decades, making her one of the few actresses to have been successful in every era of Hollywood.

Søren Kierkegaard (Philosopher)

- **Father of Existentialism:**Kierkegaard is widely regarded as the founder of existentialism, a philosophy centered on individual existence and freedom.
- **Pseudonymous Works:**He often wrote under pseudonyms to represent different aspects of his philosophy, with over two dozen different pseudonyms used throughout his works.
- **Religious Influence:**Deeply religious, Kierkegaard challenged the prevailing norms of Christianity in his time, emphasizing the need for personal faith and self-examination.

- **Broken Engagement:** His painful broken engagement to Regine Olsen significantly influenced his writing, and he never married.
- **Prolific Writer:** Despite dying at just 42, he authored more than 20 books and a large number of articles, on topics ranging from theology and psychology to literature and ethics.
- **Danish Icon:** Kierkegaard was Danish and wrote all his works in Danish, contributing significantly to Danish literature and philosophy.
- **Satirical Writings:** He also had a satirical side, often using irony and humor to criticize the establishment and society.
- **"Knight of Faith":** In "Fear and Trembling," Kierkegaard introduces the concept of the "Knight of Faith," an individual who places absolute trust in God and embraces the absurdity of life.
- **Concept of Despair:** In "The Sickness Unto Death," he presents his profound exploration of the concept of despair, which he considered the sickness of the human spirit.
- **Personal Journals:** Kierkegaard's extensive personal journals and papers, published posthumously, offer deep insights into his life and thought process, making him one of the most intensely studied philosophers.

King Tutankhamun (Pharaoh)

- **Boy King:** Tutankhamun ascended the Egyptian throne when he was only around nine years old, a fact that often leaves historians stunned.

- **Short-lived:** Known as the "Boy Pharaoh," he ruled for about ten years only, dying unexpectedly at around 18 years of age, which is astonishingly young for a ruler.
- **Tomb:** His tomb, discovered by Howard Carter in 1922, was one of the most well-preserved and intact pharaonic tombs ever found in the Valley of the Kings.
- **Artefacts:** The tomb of Tutankhamun contained an estimated 5,398 artifacts, including the iconic gold burial mask, all meant to help him in his afterlife, which is a treasure trove for archaeologists.
- **Cause of Death:** His cause of death is a subject of great debate, with theories ranging from murder to complications from a broken leg, and even a chariot accident.
- **Genetic Study:** A 2010 DNA study showed that Tutankhamun's parents were brother and sister, a surprise insight into royal inbreeding in ancient Egypt.
- **Name Change:** He originally ascended to the throne as Tutankhaten, meaning "the living image of Aten," but changed his name to Tutankhamun, "the living image of Amun," reflecting religious shifts during his reign.
- **Restoration of Polytheism:** Tutankhamun is known for reversing the monotheistic reforms of his predecessor Akhenaten, thereby restoring the worship of multiple gods in Egypt.
- **Iconic Mask:** The golden death mask of Tutankhamun is one of the most famous and beautiful works of art from the ancient world, enchanting audiences worldwide with its intricate details and historical significance.
- **Curse of the Pharaohs:** His tomb is associated with the myth of the "Curse of the Pharaohs," as several of

those who were present at the tomb's opening died under supposedly mysterious circumstances.

Lata Mangeshkar (Singer)

- **Longevity:** With a singing career spanning over seven decades, Lata Mangeshkar is one of the most enduring voices in Indian music history.
- **World Record:** Lata holds the Guinness World Record for the most recorded artist in music history, with thousands of songs to her credit.
- **Versatility:** She has sung in over 36 Indian and foreign languages, showcasing her linguistic versatility.
- **Prestigious Awards:** Lata is the recipient of the Bharat Ratna, India's highest civilian honor, and the Dadasaheb Phalke Award, the highest award in Indian cinema.
- **Cinema Legacy:** The iconic song "Aye mere watan ke logon," performed by Lata, moved India's first prime minister, Jawaharlal Nehru, to tears and has since been deeply intertwined with Indian nationalism.
- **Music Family:** She belongs to a prominent musical family, with siblings like Asha Bhosle, Usha Mangeshkar, and Hridaynath Mangeshkar, who are renowned artists in their own right.
- **Self-Taught:** Lata Mangeshkar, despite having only formal education up to the fifth grade, has written and composed songs in Marathi, demonstrating her self-taught musical prowess.
- **Nicknamed "Nightingale":** Due to her melodious voice, she was often referred to as the "Nightingale of India."

- **Reel to Real:** Several characters in Indian films have been modeled on Lata Mangeshkar's life, paying tribute to her unparalleled impact on Indian cinema and music.
- **Dedicated Philanthropist:** Lata established the Master Deenanath Mangeshkar Hospital in Pune, India, demonstrating her dedication to philanthropy and public service.

Leonardo da Vinci (Artist)

- **Proportions Guru:** He was the creator of the iconic "Vitruvian Man," which represents the perfect geometric proportions of the human body.
- **Master of Invention:** Leonardo had a mind teeming with inventions, from a helicopter prototype to a musical instrument using water.
- **Famed Artwork:** His painting, the "Mona Lisa," is one of the most recognizable and highly valued artworks in the world.
- **Mirror Writer:** Da Vinci was known to write his notes in mirror-image cursive, possibly to prevent his ideas from being stolen or simply because he was left-handed.
- **Diverse Interests:** His studies covered a wide range of topics, including anatomy, zoology, botany, geology, optics, aerodynamics, and hydrodynamics.
- **Codex Collector:** Leonardo's extensive notebooks, known as "codices," contain thousands of pages of his sketches, observations, and theories.
- **Anatomy Expert:** He performed detailed anatomical studies, even dissecting human bodies to understand their structure, a practice unusual for his time.

- **Ambidextrous:** Leonardo was ambidextrous and could write with one hand while drawing with the other.
- **Unfinished Works:** He often left projects unfinished, with his most famous incomplete work being the statue of a horse for the Duke of Milan.
- **Vegetarian:** According to several accounts, Leonardo was a vegetarian for ethical reasons, showing a deep empathy for animals.

Lin-Manuel Miranda (Composer, Lyricist)

- **Multi-Talented Genius:** Lin-Manuel Miranda has a multifaceted career as a playwright, actor, and composer, known best for creating and starring in the Broadway musicals 'In the Heights' and 'Hamilton.'
- **Inspired by Biography:** Miranda's 'Hamilton,' a groundbreaking hip-hop musical about Founding Father Alexander Hamilton, was inspired by a 2004 biography he read on vacation.
- **Notable Awards:** Miranda is a recipient of multiple prestigious awards including three Tony Awards, three Grammy Awards, an Emmy Award, and a Pulitzer Prize.
- **Remarkable Influence:** He was listed as one of Time magazine's 100 most influential people in the world in both 2016 and 2018.
- **Disney Collaborations:** Miranda contributed music, lyrics, and vocals to the soundtrack of the 2016 Disney film 'Moana,' earning him an Oscar nomination.
- **Genius Grant Recipient:** In 2015, Miranda received the MacArthur Fellowship, often referred to as the "genius grant."

- **Charitable Heart:** Miranda is also known for his activism, particularly in advocating for stronger government support for Puerto Rico, his parents' homeland.
- **Dramatic Enthusiast:** In high school, Miranda co-founded a comedy hip-hop group called 'Freestyle Love Supreme,' which later turned into a Broadway show.
- **Historic Performance:** Miranda and the cast of 'Hamilton' performed at the White House in 2016, highlighting the cultural impact of the Broadway sensation.
- **Education Advocate:** He worked with the New York City Department of Education in 2016 to ensure 20,000 public high school students from low-income families could see 'Hamilton.'

Lucille Ball (Actress)

- **TV Comedy Queen:** Known as the "Queen of Comedy," Lucille Ball starred in the groundbreaking 1950s sitcom "I Love Lucy," portraying the lovable and ambitious housewife Lucy Ricardo.
- **Historic Pregnancy:** Ball was one of the first actresses to depict a pregnancy on television, challenging societal norms and causing a big stir at the time.
- **Desilu Innovator:** Alongside her husband, Desi Arnaz, Ball co-founded Desilu Productions, which became one of the largest independent television production companies.

- **Showbiz Pioneer:** She was the first woman to run a major television studio, breaking barriers in a male-dominated industry.
- **Star Trek Sponsor:** Desilu Productions was responsible for greenlighting the original "Star Trek" series, thus Ball played an indirect but significant role in the birth of the iconic franchise.
- **Drama School Dropout:** Despite becoming one of the most loved comedic actresses, Ball was told she had "no talent" and was encouraged to leave her drama school in New York City.
- **Spy Suspicion:** During World War II, Ball claimed that her fillings could pick up radio signals and this lead to a temporary investigation by the government suspecting her of being a spy.
- **Trademark Look:** Her iconic red hair wasn't natural; Ball was born with brown hair and dyed it blonde when she first came to Hollywood, before eventually settling on her trademark fiery red.
- **Lifetime Achievement:** Ball was among the first recipients of the Women in Film Crystal Award in 1977, and in 1986, she was given the Lifetime Achievement Award from the Kennedy Center Honors.
- **Continued Influence:** Even after her death in 1989, Lucille Ball's influence on comedy and her pioneering role in television continues to be recognized and celebrated.

Mahatma Gandhi (Activist)

- **Law Background:** Before leading India to independence, Gandhi was a lawyer, having studied law in London and practiced in South Africa.
- **Philosophy of Nonviolence:** Gandhi is globally recognized for his philosophy of nonviolent resistance, or "Satyagraha," which influenced numerous other peaceful resistance movements around the world.
- **Spinning Wheel Icon:** He often spun his own cloth using a spinning wheel, known as a 'charkha', making it a symbol of Indian independence and self-reliance.
- **Tireless Marcher:** In protest of the British salt tax, he led the Salt March, a 241-mile journey on foot, which sparked similar nonviolent protests across India.
- **Prison Time:** Gandhi spent a total of about seven years in jail for his activism against the British rule in India.
- **Fasting as Protest:** He often used fasting as a means of political protest, his longest fast lasting 21 days.
- **Influential Writings:** Despite having no internet or social media, Gandhi's writings reached millions globally and influenced world figures like Martin Luther King Jr. and Nelson Mandela.
- **Vegetarianism Advocate:** He followed a strict vegetarian diet and even wrote a book on the subject, promoting it as a moral and ethical choice.
- **No Nobel Prize:** Despite being nominated for the Nobel Peace Prize five times, Gandhi never won the award.
- **Posthumous Recognition:** India honors him with a national holiday known as Gandhi Jayanti, and his birthday, October 2, is commemorated worldwide as the International Day of Non-Violence.

Marco Polo (Explorer)

- **Epic Journey:** Marco Polo was a Venetian merchant traveler whose travels are recorded in 'The Travels of Marco Polo,' a book that introduced Europeans to Central Asia and China.
- **Age of Adventure:** He embarked on his epic journey to Asia at the tender age of 17, along with his father and uncle.
- **Kublai Khan:** He spent 17 years in the court of Kublai Khan, the Mongol emperor of China, serving in various capacities including as a special envoy.
- **Language Skills:** Polo mastered several Asian languages and dialects during his travels, an impressive feat considering the communication challenges of his time.
- **Exotic Descriptions:** His book detailed exotic animals and customs of the East, including the first European descriptions of coal, eyeglasses, paper money, and postal service.
- **Doubts:** Some scholars question the veracity of Polo's tales, as he made no mention of notable aspects of Chinese culture such as the Great Wall, tea, or chopsticks.
- **Imprisonment:** Marco Polo was captured and imprisoned during a conflict between Venice and Genoa, and it was during this imprisonment that he dictated his travels to a fellow inmate.
- **Silk Road:** Marco Polo's journey largely followed the Silk Road, the major trading route between the East and the West during that period.
- **Cultural Exchange:** Polo's travels were instrumental in beginning the cultural exchange between the East and the West, significantly impacting the Age of Exploration.

- **Pasta Myth:** Contrary to a popular myth, Marco Polo did not introduce pasta to Italy. Pasta was already known to Italians long before Polo's travels to China.

Maria Callas (Opera Singer)

- **Revolutionary Performer:** Maria Callas, often regarded as the greatest opera singer of the 20th century, revolutionized the art form with her dramatic interpretations and vocal versatility.
- **Wide Range:** Her vocal range spanned from the high F above soprano C down to the F below middle C, allowing her to perform a wider variety of roles than most sopranos.
- **Weight Loss Transformation:** After a dramatic weight loss of almost 80 pounds in the early 1950s, Callas became an icon of glamour and style.
- **La Divina:** Known by her fans as "La Divina" (The Divine One), her passionate performances and dramatic life off-stage made her one of the most famous women in the world.
- **Bel Canto Resurrection:** Callas is credited with reviving the neglected bel canto repertoire, which requires a combination of vocal beauty, seamless legato, and virtuosic coloratura.
- **Tempestuous Personality:** Her off-stage life was just as dramatic as her performances, often characterized by her tempestuous personality and rumors of a rivalry with fellow soprano Renata Tebaldi.
- **Onassis Affair:** Her romantic life, including her long affair with shipping magnate Aristotle Onassis, often made headlines and added to her celebrity status.

- **Early Death:**Callas died at the age of 53 in Paris, leading to an outpouring of international grief.
- **Limited Recordings:**Despite her vast repertoire, Callas made surprisingly few studio recordings, making her live performances, many of which have been released on records and CDs, highly sought after.
- **Iconic Fashion:**Her iconic fashion sense and dramatic stage presence had a lasting impact, influencing generations of opera performers and enthusiasts.

Mark Twain (Writer)

- **Name Origin:**"Mark Twain" was a pen name; the writer's real name was Samuel Langhorne Clemens.
- **River Term:**The name "Mark Twain" is a riverboat term that means two fathoms deep, a safe depth for riverboats, reflecting his early years working on Mississippi riverboats.
- **Inventive Mind:**Twain was not just a writer but also an inventor, holding patents for items such as an adjustable strap and a history trivia game.
- **Astronomical Birth and Death:**He was born shortly after Halley's Comet appeared in 1835, and he died the day after it returned in 1910, just as he predicted.
- **Cat Lover:**Twain adored cats and reportedly had up to 19 at one point, often renting them while traveling.
- **The Jumping Frog:**His first widely successful story, "The Celebrated Jumping Frog of Calaveras County," was based on a story he heard at a California mining camp.

- **Adventures of Huckleberry Finn:** His novel 'Adventures of Huckleberry Finn' is often referred to as "The Great American Novel."
- **Bankruptcy and Lecture Tours:** After a series of unfortunate investments, Twain declared bankruptcy in 1894 and then embarked on worldwide lecture tours to pay off his creditors.
- **Early Adopter:** He was one of the first writers to use a typewriter, and his "Tom Sawyer" was the first novel written on one.
- **Mysterious Stranger:** Twain left an unfinished manuscript called "The Mysterious Stranger," which has been the subject of much debate among scholars, due to its bleak depiction of human nature.

Mary Shelley (Writer)

- **Teenage Trailblazer:** Shelley wrote her most famous novel, "Frankenstein," when she was just 18 years old.
- **Ghostly Inspiration:** The idea for "Frankenstein" came from a ghost story competition with her friends, including Lord Byron and her future husband, Percy Shelley.
- **Literary Lineage:** Mary was the daughter of two esteemed writers and philosophers, Mary Wollstonecraft and William Godwin.
- **Romantic Rebel:** She eloped with the already married poet Percy Bysshe Shelley when she was just 16.
- **Childhood Tragedy:** Her mother, the feminist writer Mary Wollstonecraft, died shortly after her birth, a tragedy that haunted Shelley throughout her life.

- **Personal Losses:** Shelley experienced the loss of three of her four children in infancy and early childhood, profoundly influencing her writing.
- **Survivor's Story:** Despite losing her husband in a boating accident and facing societal ostracism, Shelley continued to write and support her only surviving child.
- **Grave Robber:** After Percy's death, Shelley kept his calcified heart as a memento, which was found in her desk after her own death.
- **Pseudonymous Publishing:** "Frankenstein" was initially published anonymously, leading many to assume that Percy Shelley was the author.
- **Unorthodox Burial:** Upon her death, Shelley's son had her parents exhumed and buried with her, despite their wish to be buried elsewhere.

Maya Angelou (Writer)

- **Early Trauma:** Maya Angelou was mute for almost five years following a childhood trauma, which led her to develop a profound love for books and literature.
- **Renaissance Woman:** Angelou was a dancer, actress, composer, director, and activist, in addition to being an acclaimed writer.
- **Poetic Pioneer:** She was the first Black woman to have a non-fiction bestseller, her autobiography "I Know Why the Caged Bird Sings."
- **Presidential Poet:** Angelou recited her poem, "On the Pulse of Morning," at President Bill Clinton's inauguration in 1993, making her the first poet to do so since Robert Frost at JFK's inauguration.

- **Civil Rights Activist:** Angelou worked with both Martin Luther King Jr. and Malcolm X during the Civil Rights Movement.
- **Multilingual:** She was fluent in six languages - English, French, Spanish, Italian, Arabic, and the West African language Fanti.
- **Theatre Stint:** Angelou was the first Black woman to write and direct a movie, the 1998 film "Down in the Delta."
- **Nobel Connection:** Angelou received over 50 honorary degrees and was nominated for a Pulitzer Prize and a Tony Award, but she never won a Nobel prize - though she did teach at Wake Forest University, which is home to a large collection of Nobel Prizes.
- **Food Enthusiast:** She authored two cookbooks, adding yet another feather to her creative cap.
- **Unprecedented Honors:** In 2011, Angelou was awarded the Presidential Medal of Freedom, the highest civilian honor in the U.S., by President Barack Obama.

Mickey Mantle (Baseball Player)

- **Achievement:** Mickey Mantle is considered one of the greatest players in baseball history, with a career spanning 18 seasons, all with the New York Yankees.
- **Impressive Record:** He won seven World Series Championships and was named the American League's Most Valuable Player (MVP) three times.
- **Switch Hitter:** Mantle was one of the best switch hitters in baseball history, meaning he could bat from both the left and right sides.

- **Triple Crown:** In 1956, Mantle won the Triple Crown, leading the major leagues in batting average, home runs, and runs batted in.
- **Home Run Hero:** Mantle hit a total of 536 home runs during his career, and for a time, held the record for the most home runs hit in World Series play.
- **Rookie:** He began his major league career at the age of 19, quickly earning a reputation as a talented and fast player.
- **Injury-ridden:** Despite his impressive achievements, Mantle's career was plagued by injuries; he often played in pain but still managed to maintain a high level of performance.
- **Speed:** Early in his career, Mantle was known for his exceptional speed; he ran from home to first base in just 3.1 seconds from the left side of the plate.
- **Retirement Number:** The Yankees retired his jersey number (7) in 1969, the same year he retired from professional baseball.
- **Hall of Fame:** Mantle was inducted into the National Baseball Hall of Fame in 1974, his first year of eligibility, cementing his legacy as one of the sport's all-time greats.

Mozart (Composer)

- **Prodigy:** Wolfgang Amadeus Mozart, born in 1756 in Salzburg, showed prodigious ability from his earliest childhood, composing from the age of five and performing before European royalty.
- **Voluminous Work:** Despite his short life, Mozart was incredibly prolific, composing more than 800 works

including symphonies, concertos, chamber music, operas, and choral music.
- **Operatic Genius:** Mozart is known for creating some of the most revered operas in history, including "The Marriage of Figaro," "Don Giovanni," and "The Magic Flute."
- **Traveler:** He was a widely traveled composer, with journeys taking him to places like Vienna, Paris, London, Italy, and even the Vatican, where he performed for the Pope at the age of 14.
- **Quick Composer:** According to anecdotes, Mozart had an extraordinary ability to compose music quickly, with the opera "Don Giovanni" reportedly written in just a few weeks.
- **Mysterious Patron:** Near the end of his life, a mysterious patron commissioned Mozart to write a requiem mass, which remained unfinished at his death and has been the subject of much intrigue and speculation.
- **Freemasonry:** Mozart was a Freemason, and his music often includes Masonic elements, most notably in his opera "The Magic Flute."
- **Sudden Death:** Mozart died at the young age of 35 under unclear circumstances, leading to various theories about the cause of his death.
- **Posthumous Fame:** While Mozart was appreciated during his lifetime, his fame dramatically increased posthumously, and his music is now recognized for its technical skill, beauty, and emotional depth.
- **Film Subject:** The film "Amadeus," loosely based on Mozart's life, won eight Academy Awards in 1985, including Best Picture, cementing his cultural legacy for a new generation.

Nat King Cole (Singer)

- **Early Talent:** Nat King Cole, born Nathaniel Adams Coles, learned to play the organ from his mother, Perlina Adams Coles, who was the choir director at their church.
- **King Cole Trio:** Before he was a famous solo artist, he was part of the King Cole Trio, where he played piano and sang in a groundbreaking jazz style.
- **Multilingual Singer:** Known for his smooth and calming voice, Nat King Cole sang in multiple languages, including Spanish, French, Italian, and Portuguese, significantly broadening his international appeal.
- **Television Pioneer:** In 1956, he became the first African-American performer to host a variety TV series, "The Nat King Cole Show," although it was cancelled after a year due to lack of national sponsorship.
- **Civil Rights Activist:** He was active in the Civil Rights Movement and was one of the first African-Americans to purchase a house in the predominantly white neighborhood of Hancock Park, Los Angeles, facing significant racial backlash.
- **Unforgettable Legacy:** His daughter, Natalie Cole, also a successful singer, released a virtual duet of his song "Unforgettable" in 1991, which won three Grammy Awards.
- **Christmas Classic:** His rendition of "The Christmas Song" (also known as "Chestnuts Roasting on an Open Fire") has become one of the most enduring holiday classics.

- **Prolific Recording Artist:** Over his career, he recorded over 100 songs that became hits on the pop charts, an incredible achievement for any artist.
- **Smoking Habit:** A heavy smoker throughout his life, Cole believed it was key to maintaining his voice; tragically, he died of lung cancer at the age of 45.
- **Posthumous Recognition:** In recognition of his significant impact on music, he was inducted into both the Alabama Music Hall of Fame and the Rock and Roll Hall of Fame posthumously.

Nikola Tesla (Inventor)

- **Wireless Transmission Visionary:** Tesla was a pioneer in wireless transmission, dreaming of free energy for the whole world, which led to his experiments with the Tesla coil.
- **A Man of Patents:** Over his lifetime, Tesla accumulated around 300 patents worldwide for his inventions and technological developments.
- **Unusual Habits:** Tesla reportedly had a fear of pearls and an obsession with the number 3, often insisting on walking around a building three times before entering it.
- **Feats of Memory:** Tesla had an eidetic memory, which allowed him to memorize books and images and make calculations in his head.
- **Rivalry:** He had a famous rivalry with inventor Thomas Edison, known as the "War of the Currents," over the use of alternating current (AC) versus direct current (DC) electricity.

- **Extraterrestrial Beliefs:**Tesla claimed to have received signals from another planet, leading many to speculate he had made contact with extraterrestrial beings.
- **Earthquake Machine:**Tesla claimed to have invented a device, known as the Tesla Oscillator, which he believed could cause earthquakes.
- **Unfulfilled Projects:**One of his unfulfilled dreams was the 'Wardenclyffe Tower' project, intended for trans-Atlantic wireless telephony and broadcasting, but it never saw completion due to financial difficulties.
- **A Unit of Measurement:**Tesla's contributions to electrical engineering were honored by naming a unit of magnetic field strength after him - the 'Tesla.'
- **Death Ray Claims:**Towards the end of his life, Tesla claimed to have developed a "death ray" capable of destroying 10,000 airplanes from 250 miles away, but no such device has ever been found.

Oprah Winfrey (Media Mogul)

- **Struggles to Stardom:**Despite a childhood fraught with poverty and abuse, Oprah became one of the most influential women in the world.
- **Record Breaker:**Oprah was the first Black woman to become a billionaire, making her a trailblazer in multiple industries.
- **Empathy Expert:**Oprah's unique interviewing style, focusing on empathy and understanding, revolutionized talk-show hosting and led to countless memorable TV moments.

- **Book Booster:** With the launch of "Oprah's Book Club" in 1996, Oprah drastically increased book sales and readership across America.
- **Hollywood Honoree:** Oprah has been nominated for two Academy Awards, once for her acting in "The Color Purple" and once for producing "Selma."
- **Charity Champion:** Known for her philanthropy, Oprah has donated millions to educational causes and created the Oprah Winfrey Leadership Academy for Girls in South Africa.
- **Weight Watchers Wonder:** In 2015, Oprah bought a 10% stake in Weight Watchers and joined the company's board, causing the company's stock to double almost overnight.
- **Secret Santa:** During the famous "You get a car!" episode of her talk show, Oprah surprised every audience member with a new vehicle, making it one of the most iconic moments in television history.
- **Presidential Part:** Some speculate that Oprah's endorsement of Barack Obama in 2007 played a significant role in his winning the presidency.
- **Namesake Network:** In 2011, Oprah launched the Oprah Winfrey Network (OWN), becoming the first Black woman to own and run a television network.

Otto von Bismarck (Politician)

- **Unification Maestro:** Bismarck is renowned as the 'Iron Chancellor', who masterminded the unification of the disparate states of Germany into a powerful empire in 1871.

- **Calculated Combat:** His system of alliances and treaties, known as the Bismarckian system, delicately maintained the balance of power in Europe and kept Germany from going to war for decades.
- **Martial Metaphor:** Bismarck famously said, "The great questions of the day will not be settled by speeches and majority decisions—that was the great mistake of 1848 and 1849—but by iron and blood."
- **Social Security Pioneer:** He implemented the world's first welfare state, introducing government-run financial support for the elderly, the unemployed, and the sick in Germany.
- **Duelling Daredevil:** During his university days, Bismarck was an active duellist, which left him with a permanent scar on his cheek.
- **White Revolutionary:** Bismarck wore a white uniform in the Reichstag, the German parliament, leading to his nickname 'the white revolutionary'.
- **Linguistic Legacy:** His name is forever embedded in geographical features worldwide, such as the Bismarck Sea near Papua New Guinea and the city of Bismarck, North Dakota.
- **Porcine Protagonist:** To make fun of Bismarck's policies, French caricaturists often depicted him as a sausage, giving birth to the term "Bismarck herring" for a type of pickled herring.
- **Master Manipulator:** Bismarck's clever use of the 'Ems Dispatch', a selectively edited telegram, provoked France into declaring the Franco-Prussian War, which led to German unification.
- **Equestrian Ejection:** Despite his tough image, Bismarck was afraid of riding horses and was often

thrown off them, leading him to develop a permanent limp.

Patsy Cline (Singer)

- **Early Stardom:** Cline began performing at the age of 14 and achieved early local success in her hometown of Winchester, Virginia.
- **Big Break:** Her big break came in 1957 when she won Arthur Godfrey's Talent Scouts show, singing "Walkin' After Midnight."
- **Pioneering Female:** Patsy Cline is considered one of the first successful female country music artists, paving the way for many to come.
- **Signature Style:** Known for her rich tone, emotionally expressive style, and distinctive contralto voice, she is regarded as one of the greatest vocalists of the 20th century.
- **Enduring Hit:** "Crazy", written by Willie Nelson and performed by Cline in 1961, is often considered her signature song and has become one of the most covered country songs in history.
- **Tragic Demise:** At the peak of her fame, she died in a plane crash in 1963 at the age of 30.
- **Posthumous Fame:** She experienced significant posthumous recognition and was one of the first women inducted into the Country Music Hall of Fame.
- **Fashion Sense:** Patsy Cline was also known for her unique fashion sense, particularly her signature cowgirl attire with fringe dresses.
- **Biographical Film:** Jessica Lange played Patsy Cline in the 1985 biographical film "Sweet Dreams," which

focused on the singer's career and her relationship with her husband, Charlie Dick.
- **Stolen Records:**After her death, it was discovered that Patsy Cline had been cheated out of hundreds of thousands of dollars in record sales, a reality sadly common for musicians of her era.

Peter Sellers (Actor)

- **Inspector Clouseau:**Peter Sellers is best known for his role as the bumbling Inspector Clouseau in the "Pink Panther" movie series.
- **Variety of Roles:**In the film "Dr. Strangelove," he played three different roles: President Merkin Muffley, Dr. Strangelove, and Group Captain Lionel Mandrake.
- **Early Beginnings:**Sellers began his acting career as a teenager, performing comedy sketches during World War II for the Royal Air Force.
- **Radio Fame:**He shot to fame with "The Goon Show," a radio comedy series, where he showcased his ability to mimic voices and create unforgettable characters.
- **Heart Issues:**Sellers survived multiple heart attacks in his 30s and 40s but eventually succumbed to one at age 54.
- **Prolific Performer:**Despite his relatively short life, Sellers appeared in more than 60 films and numerous radio and television shows.
- **Oscar Nominee:**He was nominated for the Best Actor Oscar three times but never won the award.
- **Passionate Collector:**Sellers was an avid collector of watches and cars, owning over 80 luxury cars at one point in his life.

- **Notoriously Difficult:** Despite his on-screen charm, Sellers had a reputation for being difficult to work with, often clashing with directors and co-stars.
- **Born Performer:** Born Richard Henry Sellers, he adopted the name "Peter" after his favorite character from the novel "Peter Pan".

Queen Elizabeth II (Monarch)

- **Record-breaking Monarch:** Queen Elizabeth II is the longest-reigning current monarch, having ascended the throne on February 6, 1952.
- **World War II Service:** During World War II, she trained as a driver and mechanic, becoming the first female member of the royal family to serve in the armed forces.
- **Royal Stamps:** She is the first British Monarch to have her image printed on a postage stamp.
- **Historic Travels:** Queen Elizabeth II is the most widely traveled head of state in history, having visited more than 120 countries during her reign.
- **First Televised Coronation:** Her coronation on June 2, 1953, was the first to be televised and was watched by over 20 million people in the UK alone.
- **Loves Corgis:** The Queen has owned more than 30 corgis during her reign, all of whom are descendants of Susan, a corgi she received for her 18th birthday.
- **Multilingual Monarch:** She speaks fluent French and often uses the language for audiences and state visits.
- **Passionate Horsewoman:** Queen Elizabeth II is an avid horse rider and breeder; she has owned and bred many successful racehorses.

- **Technologically Advanced:**She sent her first email in 1976 from an army base, making her one of the earliest adopters of this technology.
- **Remarkable Longevity:**Born on April 21, 1926, Queen Elizabeth II is the oldest reigning monarch in British history.

Rachel Carson (Marine Biologist)

- **Pioneering Environmentalist:**Rachel Carson is often credited with starting the modern environmental movement with her book "Silent Spring".
- **Eye-Opening Publication:**Her groundbreaking book "Silent Spring", published in 1962, highlighted the dangers of pesticide use, notably DDT, to the environment.
- **Respected Scientist:**Before becoming a full-time writer, Carson was a respected scientist and editor with the U.S. Bureau of Fisheries.
- **Trailblazing Writer:**She was one of the first popular writers to present complex scientific ideas in a way that the general public could understand and appreciate.
- **Courageous Advocate:**Despite facing extensive criticism and backlash from chemical companies following the publication of "Silent Spring", Carson continued her advocacy for the environment.
- **Posthumous Honor:**Carson was posthumously awarded the Presidential Medal of Freedom by President Jimmy Carter in 1980.
- **Legacy Influence:**She has been honored with a Google Doodle and has had numerous schools, parks, and wildlife refuges named in her honor.

- **Beloved Works:**Her earlier books about marine life, "The Sea Around Us", "Under the Sea Wind", and "The Edge of the Sea", were bestsellers and received critical acclaim.
- **Educational Background:**Carson graduated from the Pennsylvania College for Women (now Chatham University) in 1929 and later studied at the Woods Hole Marine Biological Laboratory.
- **Fearless Challenger:**Despite suffering from ailments including breast cancer, Carson testified before Congress in 1963 on the need for new policies to protect human health and the environment.

Rembrandt (Painter)

- **Productive Artist:**Rembrandt created around 300 paintings, 300 etchings, and 2,000 drawings during his career.
- **Night Watch:**His most famous painting, "The Night Watch," is known for its large size and dramatic use of light and shadow.
- **Self-portraits:**Known for his self-portraits, Rembrandt produced nearly 100 over his lifetime, providing a detailed visual biography of his face.
- **Golden Age:**He was one of the most important figures in Dutch art history, especially during the Dutch Golden Age in the 17th century.
- **Financial Trouble:**Despite his success, Rembrandt suffered from financial difficulties and had to sell his house and works.

- **Master of Chiaroscuro**:Rembrandt is praised for his innovative use of chiaroscuro - the contrast between light and dark.
- **Personal Tragedy**:He faced numerous personal tragedies, including the death of his wife and three of their four children.
- **Art Lessons**:Rembrandt was a teacher as well as a painter and taught some of the most important Dutch painters of the time.
- **Mysterious Illness**:Towards the end of his life, Rembrandt's style changed significantly, possibly due to a condition that affected his vision.
- **Posthumous Recognition**:Although Rembrandt faced hard times later in life, his work gained enormous posthumous fame, and he is now regarded as one of the greatest visual artists in history.

Rita Hayworth (Actress)

- **Dancing Prodigy**:Rita Hayworth was a professionally trained dancer who used her dance background to transition into a successful acting career.
- **Pin-Up Icon**:She was one of the most popular pin-up girls during World War II, with her image even adorning the side of a B-29 Superfortress bomber.
- **Columbia Pictures**:Often known as the "Love Goddess," Hayworth was the top star at Columbia Pictures during the 1940s.
- **Red Hair**:Despite her famous red hair, Rita Hayworth was naturally a brunette and had her hairline raised via painful electrolysis sessions to create her signature look.

- **'Gilda'**: Her most iconic role was as the title character in the 1946 film "Gilda," in which her black satin dress and sultry performance became Hollywood legends.
- **Famous Quote**: She is credited with the quote: "Men fell in love with Gilda, but they wake up with me," reflecting the disparity between her on-screen persona and her real life.
- **Marriages**: Hayworth was married five times, including to notable figures like director Orson Welles and Prince Aly Khan, son of the Aga Khan.
- **Alzheimer's**: Hayworth was one of the first public figures to be diagnosed with Alzheimer's disease, bringing significant public attention to the condition.
- **Cultural Impact**: Her glamorous image has been referenced in numerous songs, including Madonna's "Material Girl" and the Eagles' "Hotel California."
- **Spanish Heritage**: She was born Margarita Carmen Cansino, and her father was a Spanish flamenco dancer, influencing her early dance training and career.

Robert Oppenheimer (Physicist)

- **Atomic Age**: Oppenheimer is often called the "father of the atomic bomb" for leading the Manhattan Project, the program that developed the first nuclear weapons during World War II.
- **Crisis of Conscience**: After witnessing the destructive power of the weapon he helped create, Oppenheimer famously quoted from the Hindu scripture Bhagavad Gita, saying, "Now I am become Death, the destroyer of worlds."

- **Physics Prodigy:** He was accepted at Harvard at the age of 18 and completed his chemistry degree in three years.
- **Language Love:** Oppenheimer was a lover of languages, with knowledge of eight including Sanskrit, the classical language of India.
- **Post-War Regret:** Following the bombings of Hiroshima and Nagasaki, Oppenheimer expressed regret over the development of nuclear weapons and campaigned for international control of atomic energy.
- **Security Controversy:** Despite his significant contributions, Oppenheimer's security clearance was revoked in 1954 during the height of McCarthyism due to his previous associations with the Communist Party.
- **Director's Chair:** Oppenheimer served as the director of the Institute for Advanced Study in Princeton from 1947 until 1966.
- **Nobel Snub:** He never received the Nobel Prize, despite his significant contributions to theoretical physics and his role in the Manhattan Project.
- **Perfectionist:** Known as a demanding teacher, Oppenheimer often asked his students to solve complex problems without giving them any guidance.
- **Cultural Icon:** His story has been the subject of many books and films, and he is often referenced in popular culture for his association with the atomic bomb.

Rumi (Poet)

- **Prolific Poet:** Rumi wrote around 70,000 verses in his lifetime, creating several volumes of poetry.

- **Nomadic Life:** Born in modern-day Afghanistan, Rumi lived in multiple places across the Middle East due to his family's migrations to escape political unrest.
- **Spiritual Shift:** Rumi's transformative meeting with the wandering dervish, Shams Tabrizi, altered his spiritual path and influenced much of his later poetry.
- **Beloved by Americans:** Despite having lived in the 13th century, Rumi has been one of the best-selling poets in the United States.
- **Unique Funeral:** Rumi's funeral was attended by Muslims, Christians, Jews, Greeks, Arabs, and Persians - reflecting the wide reach of his love and tolerance.
- **The Whirling Dervishes:** Rumi's spiritual teachings inspired the formation of the Mevlevi Order, better known as the Whirling Dervishes, a Sufi order known for its distinctive dance.
- **Interfaith Inspiration:** Rumi's poetry has been embraced across diverse religions, as his messages of love and unity transcend religious boundaries.
- **Translation Transformation:** Much of Rumi's popularity in the Western world is due to the numerous English translations of his work, most notably by the poet Coleman Barks.
- **Unexpected Career:** Rumi was a jurist and a theologian before he became a poet and mystic.
- **Universal Themes:** Rumi's works explore various themes such as love, loss, existence, and the quest for spiritual enlightenment, resonating with readers globally across centuries.

Samuel Beckett (Playwright)

- **Nobel Laureate:** Beckett was awarded the Nobel Prize in Literature in 1969, despite his aversion to public honors.
- **Trilingual Writer:** He wrote in three languages: English, French, and German, often translating his works from one language to another himself.
- **"Godot" Creator:** He authored the seminal play "Waiting for Godot", a cornerstone of 20th-century theatre often associated with the "Theatre of the Absurd".
- **WWII Resistance:** During World War II, Beckett was part of the French Resistance and had to flee Paris to avoid being captured by the Gestapo.
- **James Joyce Connection:** Early in his career, Beckett was a personal assistant and friend to fellow Irish author James Joyce.
- **Cricket Lover:** Beckett was a talented cricket player and remains the only Nobel laureate to be mentioned in Wisden Cricketers' Almanack, a cricket reference book.
- **Style Evolution:** Beckett's early work was influenced by the modernist style, but he later moved towards minimalism and stark presentation of human loneliness and despair.
- **Prolific in Multiple Genres:** Along with plays, Beckett wrote novels, poems, and short stories, demonstrating his versatility.
- **Silence and Pauses:** Beckett was known for using silence and pauses in his plays as much as dialogue, adding a unique depth to his works.
- **Posthumous Performances:** His play "What Where", among others, was performed for the first time only after his death, increasing his posthumous fame.

Sigmund Freud (Psychologist)

- **Dream Expert:** Freud is commonly referred to as "the father of psychoanalysis" and was a pioneer in the study of dream interpretation, viewing dreams as a window into the unconscious mind.
- **Surprising Beginnings:** Initially, Freud trained and worked as a neurologist, but his fascination with the mind led him to develop the field of psychoanalysis.
- **Cigar Lover:** Known for his love of cigars, Freud believed they enhanced his productivity and creativity; ironically, he developed oral cancer likely due to his heavy smoking.
- **Influential Concepts:** He introduced many psychological terms that we use in everyday language today, such as 'Freudian slip,' 'Oedipus complex,' and 'repression.'
- **Controversial Theories:** Despite his significant influence, many of Freud's theories, including his views on sexuality and child development, have been widely criticized and debated.
- **Fearful of Dogs:** Despite having several dogs himself, Freud suffered from cynophobia, an intense fear of dogs.
- **Escaping the Nazis:** Freud, being Jewish, fled Austria in 1938 to escape the Nazis and spent the last year of his life in London.
- **Commitment to Work:** Even when terminally ill with cancer, Freud continued to write and work on his theories, demonstrating his commitment to his field.
- **Unique Office:** Freud's office, now a museum in London, houses his famous psychoanalytic couch, which patients would lie on during sessions.

- **Unexpected Hobby:** Freud was an avid collector of ancient artifacts, amassing over 2,000 items during his lifetime, many of which are on display in his former home, now the Freud Museum.

Søren Kierkegaard (Philosopher)

- **Father of Existentialism:** Kierkegaard is often called the "Father of Existentialism" for his significant contributions to this philosophical movement.
- **Pseudonymous Works:** Kierkegaard often used pseudonyms for his works, such as 'Johannes Climacus' or 'Anti-Climacus', to challenge the reader's perspectives.
- **Brief Life:** Despite his significant influence, Kierkegaard lived a relatively short life, dying at the age of 42.
- **Religious Satire:** He published a satirical critique of the Danish Church in his later works, leading to heated public debate.
- **Tragic Love:** His broken engagement with Regine Olsen deeply affected his personal life and work, leading to profound reflections on love, sacrifice, and faith.
- **Leap of Faith:** Kierkegaard introduced the concept of the 'leap of faith', arguing that belief in God requires embracing uncertainty.
- **Prodigious Output:** During his short life, he published more than 20 books, including philosophy, theology, and fiction.
- **A Loner:** Known for his solitary lifestyle, Kierkegaard often compared himself to a 'spy' in society, observing and critiquing from the outside.

- **Legacy in Philosophy:** His existential and theological ideas continue to influence a broad array of disciplines, including philosophy, theology, psychology, and literature.
- **Honored by Denmark:** Despite facing criticism during his lifetime, Kierkegaard is now recognized as one of Denmark's most famous thinkers, with numerous statues and commemorations dedicated to him across the country.

Søren Kierkegaard (Philosopher)

- **Father of Existentialism:** Often regarded as the first existentialist philosopher, Kierkegaard's works focused on individual existence, subjectivity, and personal choice.
- **Prolific Writer:** He authored more than a dozen books and numerous works of philosophy and theology during his short life span of 42 years.
- **Pseudonymous Author:** Much of Kierkegaard's philosophical work was published under various pseudonyms, each representing a different aspect of his thought.
- **Engagement Drama:** He broke off his engagement to Regine Olsen, an event which deeply influenced his writings and personal philosophy.
- **The Concept of Anxiety:** Kierkegaard was among the first philosophers to discuss existential anxiety, suggesting that it arises from our freedom to choose and responsibility for our actions.

- **Critique of the Church:**He was a severe critic of the Danish Lutheran Church, arguing that it had become complacent and politicized.
- **Leap of Faith:**He introduced the concept of the "leap of faith", arguing that some beliefs, particularly religious ones, go beyond rationality and must be accepted without evidence.
- **The Seducer's Diary:**In his book "Either/Or", Kierkegaard, under the pseudonym of 'Johannes the Seducer', conducts a complex, eerie seduction, reflecting his love relationship with Regine Olsen.
- **Poetic Style:**Despite being a philosopher, Kierkegaard often wrote in a literary and poetic style, making his works both profound and enjoyable to read.
- **Influence:**His ideas have had a profound influence on a wide range of fields, from theology and philosophy to literature and psychology.

Henri de Toulouse-Lautrec (Painter)

- **Moulin Rouge:**Toulouse-Lautrec is most famous for his works depicting life in bohemian Paris, especially the Moulin Rouge cabaret.
- **Disability:**Born to an aristocratic family, he had a genetic condition that caused his legs to stop growing in his early teens, resulting in a full adult height of just 4 feet 8 inches.
- **Posters:**His innovative use of lithography led to him creating some of the most recognizable posters of the 19th century, essentially revolutionizing the art of poster design.

- **Montmartre:** A fixture of the Montmartre district in Paris, Toulouse-Lautrec often depicted its inhabitants, from dancers and singers to prostitutes, in his art.
- **Alcoholism:** He struggled with alcoholism throughout his adult life, often depicted drinking in his own artworks and eventually died of complications related to his excessive drinking at the age of 36.
- **Art Nouveau:** Toulouse-Lautrec's bold, graphic style was a significant influence on the Art Nouveau movement.
- **Absinthe:** A notorious absinthe drinker, he even created a famous painting titled 'The Hangover (Suzanne Valadon)', illustrating the effects of the drink.
- **Circus Paintings:** While in a sanatorium for his alcoholism, Toulouse-Lautrec created an entire series of circus paintings based on memory and imagination.
- **Anonymous Art:** He sometimes signed his works under pseudonyms to judge the public's reception of his art independently of his established reputation.
- **Posthumous Fame:** Despite his short life, Toulouse-Lautrec produced an enormous amount of art and gained significant posthumous recognition, influencing generations of artists.

Walt Disney (Animator)

- **Oscar Galore:** Walt Disney holds the record for the most Academy Awards earned by an individual, having won 22 Oscars from 59 nominations.
- **Mouse Origin:** The iconic character Mickey Mouse was co-created by Disney and Ub Iwerks and was originally

named Mortimer, but Disney's wife suggested the name Mickey instead.
- **Disneyland:** Walt Disney created Disneyland, the world's first theme park, in 1955, imagining a place where children and their parents could enjoy their time together.
- **Steam Trains:** Disney had a deep affection for trains, an influence reflected in the prominent railroads found in Disney theme parks worldwide.
- **Voice of Mickey:** For two decades, from 1928 to 1947, Walt Disney himself was the original voice behind Mickey Mouse.
- **Snow White:** Disney produced the first full-length cel-animated feature in motion picture history, "Snow White and the Seven Dwarfs," which was a massive success.
- **Ambulance Driver:** During World War I, Disney served as an ambulance driver for the Red Cross in France.
- **Imaginations Realized:** He pioneered the development of the animatronic robot, bringing to life characters like Abraham Lincoln in Disneyland's Hall of Presidents.
- **EPCOT:** Disney conceptualized the Experimental Prototype Community of Tomorrow (EPCOT) as a futuristic city, though it was built as a theme park after his death.
- **Legacy:** Walt Disney's enduring legacy includes numerous animated films, theme parks, and the multinational mass media corporation The Walt Disney Company, which remains a significant force in global entertainment.

William Shakespeare (Playwright)

- **Bard of Avon:** Shakespeare is often referred to as the "Bard of Avon", owing to his birth and burial place in Stratford-upon-Avon, UK.
- **Impressive Oeuvre:** Over his career, he wrote approximately 39 plays, 154 sonnets, two long narrative poems, and several other verses.
- **New Words:** Shakespeare is credited with inventing or first recording hundreds of words and phrases in the English language, such as "assassination", "bump", and "lonely".
- **Lost Years:** Historians refer to the period between 1585 and 1592 as "Shakespeare's Lost Years" due to the scarcity of information about him during this time.
- **Globe Theatre:** He was one of the owners of the Globe Theatre in London, where many of his plays were first performed.
- **Noteworthy Phrase:** "All the world's a stage" is one of his most famous lines, found in the play "As You Like It".
- **Queen's Company:** His acting company was originally called Lord Chamberlain's Men, but after Queen Elizabeth I's death, they became the King's Men under King James I.
- **Lasting Influence:** Four hundred years after his death, Shakespeare's plays are performed more frequently than those of any other playwright.
- **Mystery Signature:** Shakespeare's signature varies in spelling and style in the surviving examples, leading to debates among scholars about its authenticity.
- **Cryptic Epitaph:** His gravestone carries an epitaph that is said to have been written by him, warning against moving his bones, a common practice in those days to make room for more burials.

Conclusion

As we draw the curtains on this first volume of our enthralling series, "1000 Facts About Famous Figures Vol. 1", we hope that you, as the reader, have found yourself both enlightened and entertained. These pages brought to life figures that span across centuries and disciplines, their stories interweaving a vibrant tapestry of human achievement and uniqueness.

Each fact has served as a window into the lives of these iconic individuals, revealing glimpses of their brilliance, creativity, and resilience. Their personal narratives unfolded, not just as biographical accounts, but as a testament to the human spirit's boundless capacity to strive, innovate, and transcend boundaries.

With each page, we intended to fuel your imagination and ignite your curiosity, painting a multifaceted picture of these renowned figures beyond what we commonly know. Their fascinating quirks, groundbreaking accomplishments, and profound impacts became more than just information; they became stories of inspiration.

As we conclude this volume, remember that this is only the first step in our vast journey of discovery. There is a universe of knowledge yet to be explored in the subsequent volumes. We eagerly anticipate guiding you further into this extraordinary exploration of human achievement in "1000 Facts About Famous Figures Vol. 2". Until then, let the facts you've discovered here kindle a deeper appreciation of the remarkable individuals who have shaped our world.

Daniel Scott

Printed in Great Britain
by Amazon